THE THAI COOKBOOK

Authentic Recipes for Your Kitchen

PANNIPA DIBBAYAWAN
AND GUY COX

PHOTOGRAPHS BY PER ERICSON

ANGUS
& ROBERTSON
PUBLISHERS

ANGUS & ROBERTSON PUBLISHERS

Unit 4, Eden Park, 31 Waterloo Road,
North Ryde, NSW, Australia 2113;
94 Newton Road, Auckland 1,
New Zealand; and
16 Golden Square, London W1R 4BN,
United Kingdom

First published in Australia
by Angus & Robertson Publishers in 1988
First published in New Zealand
by Angus & Robertson NZ Ltd in 1988
First published in the United Kingdom
by Angus & Robertson (UK) in 1988

Copyright © Teresa Pannipa Dibbayawan and Guy Cox, 1988

National Library of Australia
Cataloguing-in-publication data.

Pannipa Dibbayawan, 1958-
   The Thai cookbook.

   Includes index.
   ISBN 0 207 15700 6.

   1. Cookery, Thai. I. Cox, Guy, 1945-
   II. Title.

641.59593

Typeset in Bembo by Setrite Typesetters Ltd, Hong Kong
Printed in Australia by Renwick Pride Pty Ltd, Thurgoona, NSW

THE THAI COOKBOOK

Authentic Recipes for Your Kitchen

PANNIPA DIBBAYAWAN
AND GUY COX

SATEH
(Satay), recipe page 15
AH JAHD
(Pickled cucumber), recipe page 16

Contents

TOM YAM GOONG
(Hot prawn soup), recipe page 37

Acknowledgements

We must acknowledge our debt in this book to Prida and Chitt, Pannipa's parents. Prida was well known as a good cook in Thailand. Her reputation lives on in Sydney – she recently turned down a pressing request to provide bulk supplies of one of her famous desserts to a Sydney Thai restaurant. Prida is the source of much of the expertise and many of the recipes in this book, while Chitt supplied many authentic ingredients from his garden.

We must also thank the many people in Australia, England, Thailand and the west coast of the United States of America, who have tried and discussed our cooking and encouraged us in this enterprise. Special thanks go to Jenny Leary and Ellen O'Brien who acted as test chefs, trying out the recipes as they were written.

Pannipa Dibbayawan and Guy Cox

PANNIPA DIBBAYAWAN was born in Bangkok and moved to Australia in 1973. In 1982 she married Guy Cox. Pannipa has a B.Sc. in microbiology and is studying for her Ph.D.

GUY COX was born in London and moved to Australia in 1975. He has M.A. and D.Phil. degrees in botany from Oxford, and at present is a Senior Lecturer at the University of Sydney.

Pannipa and Guy live in Sydney with their young son and share a love of cooking, music, and a number of outdoor activities.

Introduction

THAI FOOD

Ten years ago a Thai restaurant in a Western country was a very rare and exotic sight found only, if at all, in major cities. Today they are so common that few people would need to travel out of their own suburb to get a Thai meal. Thai food is very much a growth industry — more and more people are eating it, both in their own countries and in Thailand (one of the world's most popular tourist destinations). Yet few are cooking it in their own homes — perhaps because they feel it is "difficult", or the ingredients are unobtainable. In fact Thai food is not at all difficult to cook and the ingredients are no problem, at least in larger cities. One reason has probably been the lack of cookbooks — until recently there were no English language Thai cookery books, and even now they are scarce and often quite expensive.

This book sets out to fill the gap with a reasonably priced, comprehensive introduction to the cuisine of Thailand. Those who have holidayed in Thailand or who know Thai food only from restaurants will find that they can cook authentic and delicious Thai meals in their own kitchens.

A THAI MEAL

A Thai dinner always consists of a selection of dishes set out on the table at the same time. One will almost certainly be a *gaeng* (Thai stew or casserole, cooked in coconut milk); the others will be a range of meat, seafood and vegetable dishes chosen to provide a balanced and varied menu using whatever is in season at the time. Each person will be served with rice, and will help himself/herself to the various dishes in turn. If there is a soup, it will be served in individual bowls for each guest at the same time as the other dishes. Some of the dishes will be hot — even fiery — others mild. Instead of salt, a bowl of *nam pla* (fish sauce) garnished with cut chillies and a squeeze of lemon juice is provided, and there will be chilli sauce for those wanting even more heat.

The meal would end with a plate of fresh fruit — cut up carefully and elaborately arranged if the meal is a formal one. Cooked desserts and sweetmeats are more often eaten as snacks — something to nibble between meals or when friends call by. For a light lunch one might have a plate of fried rice or a noodle dish — these are not normally served as part of a dinner, where the carbohydrate content is provided by the plain boiled rice.

Chopsticks are not used by the Thais except sometimes for eating noodles (noodles were introduced by the Chinese, though the Thais have made them their own). A Thai meal is eaten with spoon and fork, and *farangs* (Westerners) eating in a Thai household should remember that is regarded as ill-mannered to put the fork in one's mouth. Traditional Thai cutlery is made from bronze. It can sometimes be found in Western shops; it is expensive (less so if you can buy it in Thailand), but it gives your table setting a style surpassed only by solid silver.

Thais do not usually drink wine with meals — imported wine is expensive, and the local product is very sweet. The normal accompaniment to dinner in Thailand would be water, beer or soft drinks, though the menfolk would sometimes drink potent Mekong whisky during the meal. If you like to drink wine with Thai food (and we often do) we would recommend a fruity, but not sweet, white wine, well chilled.

THE THAI KITCHEN

A traditional Thai kitchen would seem somewhat bare to Western eyes, accustomed as we are to our gadget-crowded food workshops. Food is cooked on a simple charcoal stove (*tao tahn*) shaped like a vase, with a castellated top. The top will support an iron wok for frying, a deep pot (traditionally of brass) for soups, or a mesh griddle for grilling. A steamer would carry layers of different items in bamboo baskets. Other essential kitchen utensils would be various sizes of heavy cleavers, used for everything from slicing through chopping to mincing, and a very substantial stone *krok* (mortar) and *sark* (pestle). Nowadays, the stove in any middle-class household would of course be a conventional gas or electric cooker, and some labour-saving devices would be found, though the cleavers and mortar would still be much in evidence. Kitchen aids would probably include an electric rice cooker and perhaps an electric wok. Aluminium or stainless steel would have replaced brass for everyday cooking pots.

The very simplicity of traditional Thai cooking means that little needs to be added to an ordinary Western kitchen to cook Thai food. A good solid stone mortar and pestle would be well worthwhile, and can probably be found in your nearest large Asian supermarket. While a frypan will usually be quite adequate, a wok is better for some dishes, and is no problem if you cook on gas. For an electric stove you can get heavy aluminium woks with a non-stick coating and a flat centre to the base, which will do the job, or buy an electric wok. A steamer will help for some dishes, though a sieve or colander in a large saucepan is often a reasonable substitute. A small Japanese hibachi barbecue would give extra authenticity to grilled or *pao* (Thai-style roast) dishes, but generally a conventional grill or broiler will do well enough. Although an electric rice cooker is in no sense essential, it will save a lot of labour (and free up your stove top) if you give many Asian dinner parties. Our advice is not to rush out and spend a fortune on kitchen gadgets — try the recipes in this book first, see which ones you cook most often, and then consider if one or two extra kitchen goodies might save you time and effort.

THAI FOOD AND SPECIAL DIETS

While many Thai dishes are quite salty, and some are quite rich, Thai food can nevertheless be wholly suitable for those on Pritikin or other low-fat low-salt diets. This is because in traditional Thai cooking the dishes are essentially just sauces to be eaten with large amounts of rice, which is always cooked without salt. To lower the salt content further, the amount of *nam pla* (fish sauce) in a dish can easily be reduced without doing violence to the concept. If a low fat content is important, dishes with coconut milk should be avoided, but most other main course dishes are quite all right.

A strict vegetarian diet, however, is another problem. Although Thailand is a Buddhist country, not many Thais are vegetarian. We give a section of vegetable recipes, and another on egg dishes, as well as a couple of vegetarian curries (*Gaeng Keo Wan Taohu Gup Sai Bua* and a vegetarian version of *Gaeng Garee*); *nam prik* (hot sauce) dishes are essentially vegetable-based as well. It must be admitted, however, that many of these contain *nam pla* and *gapi* (shrimp paste). A really strict vegetarian — and few Thais would be so strict — would substitute light soy sauce for the *nam pla*. *Tua nao* (bean paste) makes a suitable substitute for *gapi*, and is indeed used for that purpose in the highland regions of Thailand where shrimps are hard to come by. (In Western countries *tua nao* is more likely to be found under its Vietnamese name "*nuoc tuong hot*", since it is in wider use in Vietnam.)

bai gaprow
(hot basil)

bai maengluk
(dog basil)

bai horapa
(sweet basil)

prik keenu
(birdseye chilli)

dried *krachai*
(lesser ginger)

fresh *ka*
(galingale)

dried *ka*

pak chee
(coriander)

takrai
(lemon grass)

dried *makrut*
(kaffir lime) peel

dried *makrut* leaves,

fresh *makrut* leaves

kreung gaend ped
(red curry paste)

kreung gaeng keo wan
(green curry paste)

makam
(tamarind) pulp

THE RECIPES IN THIS BOOK

The recipes given here fall into two groups. There are those intended to be served as part of a main meal — soups, *gaeng* (curries), fish dishes, meat and poultry dishes, egg dishes, vegetable dishes, *yam* (salads) and *nam prik* (hot sauce) dishes. The others — *ahan wahng* (starters), rice and noodle dishes, desserts — are intended to be eaten on their own, as snacks or meals in their own right.

The quantities given for the main meal recipes are based on serving a selection of four or five dishes, with plenty of plain boiled rice, as a dinner for six. For a larger party one would either cook more dishes, or scale up some of them. *Gaeng* (curries) lend themselves to scaling up — a "double-size" curry, based on one kilogram of meat, with four other dishes, would do for eight people. Scaling up some of the stir-fried dishes, on the other hand, could be tricky unless you have a very large wok or pan. Soups, of course, must be scaled up — each guest must get some — but otherwise a Thai cook would be more likely to provide an extra dish or two. The selection must, naturally, provide variety and nutritional balance. For fewer people one could serve fewer dishes, but three would be an absolute minimum. Leftovers can always be eaten another day — the curries in particular reheat well, though they tend to be hotter on the second day.

For those dishes which are meals in their own right (mainly rice and noodles) we have indicated the quantities which each will serve at the end of the recipe. With the desserts and snacks, we have again tried to give some indication of how much the recipe will make where this is not obvious.

Next comes the vexed question of heat. Many Thai dishes can be positively fiery, but in Thailand, as elsewhere, how hot a dish should be is a matter for personal taste. We have tried to be consistent: all the curries, for example, should be similar in heat, so that you can easily adjust them to your own requirements. Apart from the curries, most dishes are mild unless stated to be otherwise. The degree of heat can be adjusted by varying the type and quantity of chillies — larger chillies are milder than small ones, removing the seeds lessens the heat, and the earlier they are added during cooking the hotter the result.

Finally, although we have tried to give fairly precise quantities, sauces and spices vary in strength. Tasting, and adjusting the dish to suit yourself, is an *essential* part of Thai cooking.

NOTES ON INGREDIENTS

Many Thai ingredients will not be regular components of a Western larder, but almost all can be found without major difficulty in large cities, and more are becoming available all the time as the popularity of South-East Asian food increases. We have therefore given all our recipes in true, unadulterated Thai form, while suggesting substitutes for difficult ingredients where possible. As time goes by you should need to turn to these substitutes less and less often! There remains the problem of shopping for unfamiliar ingredients, so here and in the recipes we have tried to give enough detail (and, where appropriate, alternative names) to help you find them in the sometimes confusing world of the Asian supermarket. Many ingredients which in Thailand would be available all year round — for example, basil, coriander and mint — will be seasonal in colder climates. The Thais, however, who do not import much fruit or vegetables, are well used to adjusting their menus to the changing seasons. You should do as a Thai would do, and choose the dishes you cook to suit what is in season.

Basil

Three varieties of basil are commonly used in Thai cooking. *Bai horapa* (*Ocimum basilicum*) is the commonest, and is an essential ingredient of Thai curries and many other dishes. Botanically it is regarded as identical to the European sweet basil, but it is slightly different in appearance and flavour; it has reddish stems and mid-ribs and a slight flavour of aniseed. Many Chinese shops sell it fresh, but ordinary sweet basil can be substituted if it is unavailable.

Bai maengluk (*O. canum*) is botanically distinct from European sweet basil but has a very similar flavour. It is the variety which should be used for *Kanom Jeen Nam Ya Gai* (noodles with spicy chicken sauce, p. 28), but again sweet basil can be substituted.

Bai gaprow (*O. sanctum*) — hot basil or holy basil — has a hot spicy flavour and can be recognised by the slightly serrated edges of its leaves. It is required for some dishes — for example, *Gai Pad Bai Gaprow* (chicken with hot basil, p. 58) — and no substitute is really worth attempting.

All these varieties of basil are annuals, and can be grown easily in summer in temperate climates if protected from frost. In the tropics, of course, they will grow all year round. In Italy many different varieties of basil, neglected elsewhere in Europe, are grown and some of these could provide close equivalents for all three Thai varieties.

Cardamon (*look grawan*)
Elettaria cardamomum

Large seeds (popularly called cardamon "pods") which are an essential ingredient of *Gaeng Masaman Neuea* (Muslim beef curry, p. 46). They can be bought at Asian stores or most supermarkets.

Chilli (*prik*)
Capsicum frutescens

Botanically, all the chillies are closely related to the capsicum (*C. annuum*) or sweet bell pepper. They come in an infinite variety of forms and degree of heat. In this book we distinguish three types. Banana chillies (*prik yuok*), the large, pale green variety which are not at all hot, we regard as interchangeable with capsicum (bell pepper) for culinary purposes. The medium sized and medium heat variety (*prik chee fa*), about 10 cm long, whether red or green, are used to add spice and flavour to a dish without dominating it. When we refer to "large mild" chillies this is the type we intend. The small "birdseye" chilli (*prik keenu*) is about 3 cm long and extremely hot. It is specified in recipes where its potency is required.

In general, however, it is a matter of personal taste how hot you make any given dish. If you like it hot, use more chillies or a hotter variety. Any type of chilli is milder if you remove the seeds; also, the earlier in the cooking process at which the chillies are added, the more heat they give to the rest of the food.

Chinese chives (*gui chai*)
Allium tuberosum

Chinese chives are quite different from the Western type; their leaves are strap-like instead of tubular and they have a garlicky flavour. If you cannot get them "garlic chives" would be a better substitute than the common variety.

Coconut milk (*nam kati*)

This is a basic ingredient in much South-East Asian cooking. It has no connection with the watery fluid found inside the coconut; it is prepared by steeping the flesh of the coconut in water. There are two types: "thick", and "thin".

To prepare coconut milk the traditional way, grate the flesh of a coconut very finely. To 400 g of grated coconut (approximately one coconut), use 1 cup of boiling water. Pour the water over the coconut and let stand for 20 minutes. Squeeze out the liquid with your hands, over a fine sieve (to catch the bits of coconut you drop) — this will give you about 1½ cups of thick coconut milk. Do not throw the coconut away — repeat the process with the same grated coconut, but with 2 cups of water, to give you thin coconut milk.

Desiccated coconut can be extracted similarly, allowing approximately half the weight per cup of water that would be used with fresh coconut, but it is very definitely a poor substitute.

A simple alternative is to use tinned or "longlife" coconut milk — but make sure that it is not the sweetened kind sold for mixing in cocktails. Tinned coconut milk is thick — add approximately the same volume of water to make thin milk.

A cheaper but still simple method is to use blocks of creamed coconut, widely available in supermarkets and delicatessens: ⅓ of a block, mixed with 1 cup of boiling water, gives thick milk; ⅓ of a block with 2 cups of water gives thin milk.

Coconut milk does not keep long, even in the

fridge. Freeze any you want to keep longer than 24 hours. It will separate on freezing, but can be re-mixed when it thaws.

Coriander (*pak chee*)
Coriandrum sativum

Coriander is called "cilantro" in America, and is also sometimes labelled "Chinese parsley". Thai cooking uses the leaves, roots and seeds of this herb in a wide variety of dishes — you cannot cook a genuine Thai meal without it. The seeds are available from any supermarket and delicatessen. Bunches of the leaves are available in Chinese shops, and from the more enterprising vegetable shops. Try to find bunches with the roots still on (or train your local greengrocer).

Coriander grows easily in a sunny spot or in a pot on the windowledge; as the plant ages, the leaves change their form and become more and more divided. Only use the young, more or less entire, leaves.

Cumin (*yeera*)
Cuminum cyminum

The seeds of a plant of the family Umbelliferae (which includes coriander, celery and parsley). They are used in some curry powders and pastes and many other dishes, and are readily available from any supermarket.

Curry pastes (*kreung gaeng*)

In Thailand most households would buy their curry pastes freshly made from the local market. We do not have that option in Western countries, but they can be bought in tins or plastic packets from many Asian food stores. We give recipes for making them (pages 41 to 42) but many of the ingredients can be hard to find. Undoubtedly a homemade paste is best — but a bought paste will be both better and less effort than a paste made from substitute ingredients.

Eggplant/aubergine (*makeua*)
Solanum melongena

Various different varieties of eggplant are grown in Thailand. *Makeua yao* is the largest, and is usually green and elongated. Ordinary purple or white egg-plant can be substituted for this. Medium-sized forms, the size of small tomatoes, are *makeua proa*, *makeua kai* and *makeua kao*; these are all crispy, with a dryish flesh, and are eaten raw with *nam prik* (hot sauce) or cooked in curries. The smallest are called *makeua pooang*; these grow in bunches, are the size and shape of peas, and are used in *gaeng keo wan* (green curry) dishes.

Fish sauce (*nam pla*)

A thin, clear sauce prepared from fermented salted fish. Do not confuse it with oyster sauce, which is totally different. Fish sauce is available from any Asian food store and many suburban delicatessens.

Flour (*paeng*)

As well as ordinary wheaten flour (*paeng salee*), Thais use a range of other flours. Cornflour or cornstarch (*paeng kao paud*) is often used as a thickener, though tapioca flour (*paeng mun*) is also used for this purpose, and is specifically required in several sweet and savoury dishes. Rice flour comes in two forms, long-grain rice flour (*paeng kao jao*) and glutinous rice flour (*paeng kao neow*); these are quite different in properties and uses. Bean flour (*paeng tua*), made from soya beans, is used in desserts. All of these flours are readily available in Chinese shops, and they can often be bought at health food stores.

Soya flour from health food shops is yellower in colour than Asian bean flour, but seems to be perfectly satisfactory in Thai recipes. Rice flour from health food shops, however, is often coarsely ground and can give a granular texture to dishes which should be smooth. Glutinous rice flour in health shops, on the other hand, seems identical to that sold in Asian groceries.

Galingale (*ka*)
Alpinia galanga

A relative of ginger, galingale was once well known in Europe and England, but ceased to be imported when the sea routes opened up by the British East India Company and their counterparts in France and Portugal took over from the overland routes of the

SAKU SAI MOO
(Stuffed sago balls), recipe page 16

Old Silk Road. Galingale has rhizomes which are similar to but narrower than those of ginger, and a similar but milder flavour. It can be obtained in Eastern supermarkets in dried form, both as slices and as powder. In powdered form it is commonly known by its Indonesian name, "laos". The powder can be used in curry pastes and other pounded spice mixtures, but other recipes require the sliced form. Some shops also stock it in tins or jars, in brine or water; this can be used as a substitute for the fresh root, but rinse it well if it has been in brine.

Galingale can be grown even in temperate climates if protected from frost; it needs plenty of water and will thrive in a shady spot.

Garlic (kratiem)
Allium sativum

Thai garlic, while botanically identical to that used in the West, usually has much smaller cloves. Thai recipes therefore generally contain what seem like extreme quantities of garlic! All the recipes in this book are based on Western-sized cloves of garlic; if you are cooking them in Thailand or elsewhere in South-East Asia the number of cloves should be approximately doubled.

Kaffir lime (makrut)
Citrus hystrix

The fruit of this variety of lime is dry, sour and quite inedible, but its aromatic rind is an essential ingredient in curry pastes. It can be bought dried, in strips, in Asian shops. If you cannot get it, use lime or lemon peel.

The leaves too are used as flavouring in many dishes. These can also sometimes be bought dried, but they should not be kept too long or they lose all flavour and aroma. It is better to substitute fresh lemon leaves than to use old, tasteless dried makrut!

The tree is native to the tropics and will only grow in tropical or subtropical climates.

Lemon grass/citronella (takrai)
Cymbopogon nardus

A grass-like plant with a strong aroma and flavour of lemon. The leaf bases, chopped or pounded, are used in a wide variety of dishes. The free, green parts of the leaves are not used (except to make a brush for basting meat on the grill). The plants can often be bought fresh at Chinese shops and health food shops which sell fresh produce, and they grow easily in the garden. If you cannot get them, dried lemon grass is often available in packets in Asian supermarkets and health food stores.

Onions (horm)
Allium cepa

Thai onions, like their garlic, are much smaller than the common Western varieties. Quantities given in this book are for our large onions, and would need to be increased if Thai onions were used. Spring onions (green onions or scallions) are also used a lot in Thai cooking; they are called *ton horm* and the green part is used as well as the white.

In Australia spring onions are often, very misleadingly, called shallots. Shallots are in fact a variety of onions which are divided into cloves like garlic; they make a good equivalent for Thai onions and can be used (with an appropriate adjustment of quantities) in any of the recipes in this book which use onions.

Shrimp paste (gapi)

A thick paste prepared from shrimps and salt; it has a very strong taste (and smell). The larger Asian food stores will have the Thai variety, and you should buy this if you can. The Malay/Indonesian version (blachan or belacan) is more widely available, and can be used at a pinch, but it is much drier and has a rather different flavour.

Afer taking *gapi* from the jar, smooth the remainder down well to leave the minimum surface exposed, and it will keep well even out of the refrigerator. Keep the jar well sealed or everything in your fridge or cupboard will smell of it!

Soy beans (tua leuang)
Glycine max

These beans are used in a vast number of ways in Thai (and all Far Eastern) cooking. Fermented whole beans (*tao jiew*) are available as yellow beans (*tao jiew kao*) or black beans (*tao jiew dam*); both of these can

KANAH PAD NAM MUN HOY
(Broccoli with oyster sauce), recipe page 72
PAD FUK TONG, and NAM PRIK SIRACHA
(Fried pumpkin, recipe page 71, and Siracha chilli sauce, recipe page 84)

KAI LOOK KOEI
(Son-in-law eggs), recipe page 65

be bought in tins in any shop which sells Chinese food. Whole beans can also be roasted like peanuts and eaten as an appetiser. Soy flour is used for desserts. Fermented soy beans are used to make soy sauce, which comes in two forms, dark and light. A thicker version is black bean sauce, while *tua nao* (a very thick paste) is used in regions of Thailand remote from the sea as an alternative to *gapi* (shrimp paste). Various forms of *taohu* (bean curd) — often known by the Japanese name "tofu" — are also prepared from soy beans. The beans are also pressed to extract oil.

Sugar (*nam tan*)

While cane sugar is now common in Thailand, traditional Thai sugar — palm sugar — is obtained from a species of palm tree. This comes in a variety of forms — dry cakes or a thick paste in jars, and dark brown to cream in colour. Unless recipes specify white sugar, palm sugar is definitely the best sort to use if your Asian shop has it. The lighter-coloured form is the type commonly sold in Thailand, and the palest sort can even be used in desserts which specify (for reasons of colour) white sugar. If palm sugar is unavailable the best alternatives are raw, demerara or light brown sugar.

Swamp cabbage (*pak boong*)
Ipomoea aquatica

This is a close relative of Morning Glory and of the sweet potato (*I. batatas*). The young stalks and arrow-shaped leaves are cooked in a variety of dishes. It can often be found in Chinese shops under the name of *ong choi*, but spinach makes an acceptable substitute.

Swamp cabbage can be grown as an annual crop in temperate climates, but needs to be protected from frost. It requires both plenty of sun and plenty of water.

Tamarind (*makam*)
Tamarindus indica

Tamarind fruits are borne in brownish pods on a large, ornamental tree with distinctive feathery leaves. The fruits have a pulpy coating around one or two seeds, and the less sour varieties can be eaten fresh when ripe. They are also turned into sweets, in Thailand, by preserving with sugar.

The pulp, used to give a sharp taste to a wide range of dishes, can be bought in packets, and is used to make tamarind water. This is made by stirring 1 tablespoon of pulp into 1 cup of boiling water; allowing 5 minutes for it to infuse then straining off the water from the stringy remains of the pulp. Alternatively, a concentrated extract (resembling yeast extract in appearance) can be bought in jars; 1 teaspoon of this is equivalent to 2 tablespoons of tamarind water.

Turmeric (*kamin*)
Curcuma domestica

Turmeric is a rhizome in the same family as ginger and galingale. It has a mild flavour and a strong yellow colour. It is available anywhere in powder form, and is used in curry powder and soups; the Thais also use it fresh, but this is not so easy to find in Western countries.

Appetisers and Snacks

Ahan wahng

Appetisers and Snacks – Ahan wahng

In a Thai house, starters such as these would be served to the guests *before* they sat down to the dinner table. The name *ahan wahng* literally means "food while you are doing nothing". Once the party sits down to dine, the rice and main courses would be served — the serious eating has begun. *Ahan wahng* are equally likely to be eaten as snacks or light meals — at almost any time of day.

SATEH

SATAY

1 kg beef, pork or chicken fillet
3 stalks lemon grass
½ small onion
1 clove garlic
1 teaspoon curry powder (Pong Garee, see p. 43)
3 teaspoons coriander seeds
3 teaspoons sugar
A pinch of salt
3 teaspoons nam pla (fish sauce)
4 tablespoons water
Thin coconut milk for basting (see p. 7)
Wooden satay sticks (12–13 cm long)

Peanut sauce:

75 g roasted, unsalted peanuts
1 teaspoon Kreung Gaeng Ped (red curry paste, see p. 42)
200 mL thick coconut milk (see p. 7)
100 mL water
1 tablespoon sugar
½ teaspoon salt
3 tablespoons tamarind water (see p. 11)

Garnish:

Ah Jahd (pickled cucumber, see p.16)

The satay sticks should be 12–13 cm long — if you can only get long kebab sticks break each into two. One kilogram of meat will make around 70 satay sticks — for an appetiser, 5–6 sticks per person would be enough; 10–12 would make a main course.

Cut the meat (beef, pork, chicken or a mixture) into thin strips about 10 cm long by 2–3 cm wide and put aside. Chop the lemon grass into slices, peel and coarsely chop the onion and garlic. Throw these into a blender with the curry powder, coriander seeds, sugar, salt, *nam pla* and water and blend till smooth. Marinate the meat in this mixture for 2–3 hours. Thread the pieces of meat onto satay sticks, one per stick. Do not waste shorter pieces of meat — just put two or three together on a stick.

Pound the peanuts to a grainy paste in a mortar. Mix the curry paste with 3 tablespoons of the coconut milk and cook in a saucepan until it is frying and smells cooked (about 2–3 minutes). Add the remainder of the coconut milk, and the water, and bring to the boil, then add the remaining peanut sauce ingredients. Adjust to taste with more tamarind water or salt if necessary, and simmer for 5 minutes.

Cook the satay sticks on a barbecue or under a grill, basting generously with coconut milk. Traditionally the brush for this is a bundle of lemon grass leaves, and if you have used fresh lemon grass for the marinade you might as well follow tradition! (Only the fleshy bases of lemon grass stalks are used in cooking.)

Dip the satay sticks in the peanut sauce when you eat them, and serve *Ah Jahd* (pickled cucumber, see p. 16) as a side-dish.

Appetisers and Snacks – Ahan wahng

SAKU SAI MOO

STUFFED SAGO BALLS

1 cup sago
$\frac{1}{4}$ cup warm water
1 teaspoon coriander roots
$\frac{1}{2}$ tablespoon oil
300 g minced pork
1 tablespoon nam pla (fish sauce)
$\frac{1}{4}$ cup raw peanuts, coarsely pounded
1 tablespoon sugar
Tapioca flour for dusting

Garlic oil topping (optional):

2 tablespoons oil
5 cloves garlic

Garnish:

Coriander leaves
Lettuce leaves

Add the water to the sago, a little at a time, and knead until soft. Leave covered with a damp cloth for 1 hour. Pound the coriander roots to a fine paste. Heat the oil in a pan, fry the coriander root paste until it smells cooked (see our note, p. 41), then throw in the pork and stir-fry for 5 minutes. Add the *nam pla*, peanuts and sugar and adjust the seasoning to taste. Stir-fry until the mixture is dry.

If the sago mixture has become hard, knead in more warm water until it is manageable. Dust your hands with tapioca flour and make uniform balls of the sago paste, 2–2.5 cms in diameter. Take a ball, work it well between your hands, and gradually flatten it into a circular sheet as thin as you can get it. Place a teaspoonful (more or less, depending on the size of your sago sheet) of the pork and peanut mix in the centre, and fold up into a ball. Cook the balls on a sheet of oiled aluminium foil (or more tradition-ally, a banana leaf) in a steamer for around 15 minutes, until the sago is translucent. If the balls touch they will stick together, so do not try to cook too many at one time.

To make the garlic oil dressing, crush the garlic, leaving some of the skin on, and fry in the oil until brown. Tip the oil and garlic into a small dish.

Serve the balls each on a piece of lettuce leaf, with a couple of drops of the garlic oil on top and a sprig of coriander alongside. This quantity of *Saku Sai Moo* makes a substantial snack for 6 people or a party dish for rather more.

AH JAHD

PICKLED CUCUMBER

1 small cucumber
1 small onion
1 large red chilli
2–3 cm piece fresh (green) ginger
1 tablespoon sugar
$\frac{1}{2}$ cup water
$\frac{1}{2}$ cup vinegar

Peel the cucumber, halve it lengthwise then slice it thinly. Peel and thinly slice the onion (lengthwise). Cut the deseeded chilli and the ginger into fine strips. Mix the sugar with the water and vinegar, mix in the cucumber, onion and ginger, and scatter the chilli on top.

Ah Jahd is served as a side-dish with *Sateh* (see p. 15) and *Gaeng Garee Gai* (see p. 46).

Appetisers and Snacks – *Ahan wahng*

YAHNG MOO

BARBECUED PORK

10 coriander roots
1 cm piece fresh (green) ginger, peeled
1 clove garlic, peeled
$\frac{1}{2}$ teaspoon peppercorns OR ground pepper
1 tablespoon nam pla (fish sauce)
1 tablespoon light soy sauce OR half and half dark soy sauce and nam pla
1 tablespoon whisky
1 teaspoon sugar (palm or raw sugar for preference)
400–500 g pork leg fillet (preferably in one piece)

Garnish:

Coriander leaves
Fresh salad vegetables

Cut the coriander roots, ginger and garlic, and place in a mortar. Add the peppercorns and pound to a coarse paste. Add the sauces, whisky and sugar and mix well. (You could substitute sherry for the whisky, and omit the sugar.) Slice the meat thinly, pour the marinade over it, and stir well. Leave to marinate for a minimum of 30 minutes — an hour would be better.

Brush your grill pan with oil, lay out the pork slices on it and grill under maximum heat until cooked — about 5 minutes per side. Alternatively (and more authentically), grill on a barbecue.

Serve garnished with coriander leaves and fresh, sliced salad vegetables, as available.

The quantity given here could be served as one of the dishes at a dinner for 6. As an appetiser or party dish it would serve 10–12. It could be made with beef — in which case it would be *yahng neuea* — or with calves' liver (*dap yahng*). Another version, using beef, is given on page 20.

TORD MUN PLA

FISH PATTIES

Fish:

500 g gemfish fillet (or other firm white fish)
3 teaspoons Kreung Gaeng Ped (red curry paste, see p. 42)
1 tablespoon nam pla (fish sauce)
2 snake beans OR 4–6 young green beans
Oil for deep-frying

Sauce:

3 tablespoons vinegar
1 teaspoon sugar
$\frac{1}{2}$ teaspoon salt
1 small cucumber, thinly sliced
1–2 large mild chillies, cut into fine slivers
1 tablespoon crushed unsalted peanuts

Garnish:

Coriander leaves

Remove skin and bones from the fish fillets, cut into pieces and pound in a mortar until the paste becomes quite sticky (the stickier the better). Add the curry paste and *nam pla* and mix in well. Chop the snake beans into very fine slices and mix them in too. Take a tablespoon of the mixture and roll it into a ball then flatten it into a patty. Deep-fry in oil over a medium heat until the patties are golden brown.

To make the sauce, dissolve the sugar and salt in the vinegar and mix in the cucumber, chilli and peanuts.

Garnish the sauce with coriander leaves and serve in a separate dish with the patties.

This quantity of *Tord Mun Pla* would make a generous appetiser for 6 people.

Appetisers and Snacks – Ahan wahng

POA PIA
SPRING ROLLS

Filling:
50 g peeled raw prawns (approx. 100 g whole prawns, shelled)
50 g minced pork
10 g woon sen (mung bean vermicelli)
50 g carrot, coarsely grated
50 g bean sprouts
1 spring onion, coarsely chopped
2 teaspoons light soy sauce
2 teaspoons cornflour
Water
1 packet frozen 12 cm square spring roll wrappers, thawed
Oil for deep-frying

Sauce:
2 tablespoons vinegar
2 teaspoons sugar
$\frac{1}{2}$ teaspoon salt
1 tablespoon finely grated radish

Garnish:
Coriander leaves

Mung bean vermicelli (bean vermicelli) is available at any Asian shop and many delicatessens and super-markets.

Spring roll wrappers come in packets, frozen, at any Chinese grocery and many delicatessens. Thai (and other South-East Asian) spring rolls always use the small-size wrappers; if you can only get the large Chinese sort cut each one in four. The packet must be properly thawed before you attempt to peel off the wrappers from the pile. The remaining wrappers can be re-frozen, but always seal them in a freezer bag first; if they dry out they are useless.

Chop the prawn meat finely and mix with the minced pork. Break up the vermicelli into 3–5 cm pieces and soak in hot water for 10 minutes. Mix the carrot and the bean sprouts in with the meat. Drain the vermicelli, and add to the mixture with the spring onion. Stir in the soy sauce.

Mix the cornflour with a little water to make a thin paste — this is used to seal up the rolls. Open the packet of spring roll wrappers. Although they are in a sealed packet, you may find that the outer ones are dry, in which case you will find it much easier to split the stack in the middle and peel them off from there. Take only one wrapper at a time, and keep the remainder covered with a damp cloth. Lie the wrapper down, diamond-wise, and fold the top corner in the centre. Place some of the filling (about 2 teaspoons) on the doubled-over part. Fold in the left and right corners, then roll over, downwards. Paint some of the cornflour and water over the bottom corner before rolling it all up. Continue making rolls until all the filling is used up — the quantity given here will make between 15 and 20 rolls, depending on how generous you are with the filling.

Pour the oil in a frying pan or deep-fryer to a depth of 2.5 cm, and heat. Fry the rolls, a few at a time, until they are golden brown. A medium heat should be used — if the oil is too hot the wrapper will brown instantly, before the filling is cooked, but if they take more than 3–4 minutes they will become soggy. Turn them during cooking so that they colour evenly.

To make the sauce, mix the vinegar, sugar, salt and radish and adjust the seasoning to taste. Traditionally the long white Chinese radish should be used, but we prefer the red European kind — they are both different varieties of the same species, anyway.

Serve the spring rolls on a plate with the sauce in a dish at the centre, and scatter a few coriander leaves over the top.

Appetisers and Snacks – *Ahan wahng*

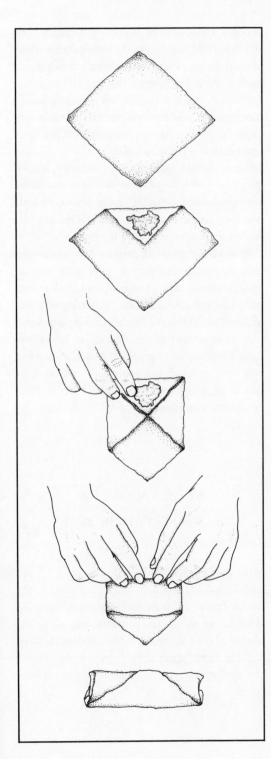

TAOHU TORD
TOFU CHIPS WITH DIP

Tofu chips:
250 g bean curd (tofu)
Oil for deep-frying

Dip:
3 cloves garlic
6 coriander roots
10 peppercorns
200 mL thick coconut milk (see p. 7)
100 mL water
100 g minced pork
100 g minced raw prawn meat
2 tablespoons palm (or raw) sugar
1 tablespoon nam pla (fish sauce)
1 tablespoon raw peanuts, pounded OR *crunchy peanut butter*
1 tablespoon lime (or lemon) juice

Cut the bean curd (the more solid type of fresh bean curd is best for this) into 3 mm thick slices. Heat oil in a pan, and deep-fry the tofu pieces on a good heat, turning from time to time, until they are crispy and coffee-coloured. Do not try to do too many at once or they will stick together. Drain on paper towels.

To make the dip, pound together the "heavenly" spices (garlic, coriander roots and peppercorns) to a fine paste. Bring the coconut milk and water to the boil and keep at a moderate boil for 5 minutes. Stir in the paste, add the pork and prawns and cook for about 5 minutes. Add the sugar, *nam pla* and peanuts and adjust to taste. Simmer uncovered for 10 minutes, then stir in the lime juice and remove from the heat.

Serve the tofu chips while warm, with the dip in a separate bowl.

Appetisers and Snacks – *Ahan wahng*

HOY TORD

MUSSEL PANCAKE

1 kg fresh mussels
OR *200 g shelled mussels*
3 tablespoons tapioca flour
1 tablespoon rice flour
4 tablespoons water
Oil for frying
1 egg
1 clove garlic, chopped
1 cup bean sprouts, washed
2 spring onions, cut into 1 cm lengths
1 tablespoon nam pla (fish sauce)

Garnish:

5 sprigs coriander
Coarsely ground black pepper
Nam Prik Siracha (Siracha chilli sauce, see p. 84)
Prik Nam Som (chillies in vinegar, see p. 84)

One kilogram of fresh mussels will yield about 200 g meat — you can save labour by buying shelled mussels, though these have usually been frozen. Other shellfish could also be used — small clams, cockles or oysters.

Wash the mussels and remove the "beards". Steam them, or heat in large saucepan with a little water, until they are just open. Remove the meat. Mix the tapioca and rice flours, and stir in the water spoonful by spoonful. Add the mussels.

Heat a generous tablespoon of oil in a 25 cm (or larger) frypan; the oil is hot enough when a drop of the flour and water mix puffs up immediately when dropped in. Tip in the flour and mussel mixture. When the base has set but the top is still runny, break the egg on top and stir it around to blend the yolk and white and mix it with the top layers of the batter. Spoon oil from the sides of the pan over to help the top to set. When the base is brown and the middle is beginning to set, flip the pancake over to cook the top. (If you are nervous about this, slide it

out onto a plate then tip it over onto another plate and slide it back into the pan. An extra half tablespoon of oil in the pan before you put it back in might be a good idea if you are doing it this way.) If you decide you have flipped it too soon it will not hurt to turn it back again — this omelette-pancake hybrid is surprisingly robust and easy to handle. When it is cooked, slide it out onto a plate.

Put a little more oil in the pan if necessary, and fry the garlic until it is golden brown, then toss in the bean sprouts and the spring onions. Stir over a high heat for a couple of minutes, then add the *nam pla*. Stir briefly then remove from the heat.

Spread the bean sprout mixture over a plate and serve the pancake (egg side up) on top of the sprouts. Sprinkle the top with coarsely ground black pepper and scatter coriander leaves over it. Serve with a dish of *Nam Prik Siracha* and another of *Prik Nam Som*.

As an appetiser this size pancake can be cut into segments to serve 4–6 people. It is equally good as a light meal, in which case you would cook one pancake, using half this quantity per person, and increase the amount of mixture accordingly.

NEUEA NAM TOK

WATERFALL BEEF

Make as *Yahng Moo* (barbecued pork, see p. 17) but with 2 small hot red (birdseye) chillies added to the pounded paste, and using beef steak (rump or equivalent) as the meat. You can of course adjust the amount of chilli to taste, but it is intended to be very hot. The name "waterfall beef" refers to the amount of water (or beer) needed to quench the fire in your mouth.

Light Meals
Rice and Noodles

Light Meals – Rice and Noodles

Rice is the centerpoint of a Thai meal. "*Gin kao mai*" — "Will you eat rice?" is an expression you are bound to hear if you visit a Thai household, and it means, "Will you stay to dinner?" Except in the most humble family the meal would consist of much more than rice, but the expression sums up the central role played by rice. Many Thai dishes are very hot and often quite salty, but they are all intended to be eaten as a sauce with plenty of plain boiled rice, which is always cooked without salt.

More complex rice dishes are not served as part of a main meal; they are light meals in their own right and would be eaten as lunch or supper dishes. *Kao pad* (fried rice) or noodles, often bought at a roadside cafe or from a travelling vendor, make an ideal lunch in the Thai climate. Rice soup (*kao tom*, or *jorg*) is a light breakfast or an "anytime" snack.

How to make plain boiled rice (*kao*)

Many Thai families nowadays have an electric rice cooker, and it cannot be denied that it makes cooking an Asian meal much simpler if you have one. You just put in the number of measures of rice you require, fill with water to the appropriate line, and switch on. It is still useful, however, to know how to cook good rice without such aids.

The traditional Thai way of cooking rice is by the absorption method. Allow half a cup of rice per person, and wash the rice well in a sieve under running water. Shake out as much as possible of the water and put the rice in a heavy saucepan. Add 4 cups of cold water for each 3 cups of rice. Put on a low heat and allow to come to the boil, then cook (with the heat as low a possible) until all the water is absorbed. This will take around 20 minutes. Turn off the heat and leave in the saucepan on the back of the stove until you are ready to eat.

A useful alternative if you are short of time is the rapid boil method. This requires a much larger saucepan for the same quantity of rice. Wash the rice as above, then throw into a large pan of boiling water. Keep it boiling vigorously until the rice is cooked, which in this case will be only about 5 minutes. Strain the rice and immediately wash with cold running water (to stop the cooking process). Finally, rinse with a kettle of boiling water to warm the rice again, and serve.

KAO TOM MOO

RICE SOUP

200 g pork fillet
1 tablespoon oil
3 cloves garlic, chopped
4 cups stock or water
1 large coriander plant (stalks and leaves), chopped
5 spring onions, chopped
2 tablespoons nam pla (fish sauce)
1 tablespoon vinegar
4 cups cooked rice (see above)

Cut the pork into small, thin slices, about 1 cm × 2 cm and 2 mm thick. Heat the oil in a large saucepan and fry the pork and garlic until brown. Add the stock and simmer for 10 minutes or until the meat is cooked. Add the coriander, spring onions, *nam pla* and vinegar, then stir in the rice. Adjust the seasoning to taste and serve immediately. (If it is left too long the rice will soak up a lot of the stock.)

Chicken or fish can be used instead of pork, with appropriate adjustments to the cooking times. This is a very popular breakfast in Thailand but could equally well be served as a light lunch or supper; it is a handy way of using up leftover rice. The quantity given here serves 3 or 4 people.

Light Meals – Rice and Noodles

KAO MUN GAI

RICE AND CHICKEN

Chicken:

2 coriander roots, roughly pounded
700 g chicken breast (3 half breasts), bone included
5 cups water
1 teaspoon salt

Rice:

4 cloves garlic, peeled
1 tablespoon oil
2½ cups rice

Sauce:

1 teaspoon green (fresh) ginger (a piece about 2 cm long)
1 large red chilli
1 tablespoon tinned black beans
1 tablespoon sugar
1 tablespoon nam pla (fish sauce)
1 tablespoon dark soy sauce
1 tablespoon vinegar

Garnish:

2 cucumbers, sliced
Coriander leaves

Put the chicken, water, salt and coriander roots in a saucepan, and bring to the boil. Simmer until the chicken is cooked (around 15–20 minutes, depending on the size of the breasts), skimming off the froth from time to time. Take out the chicken, reserving the stock, remove the flesh from the bone and cut into bite-size pieces.

Bruise the garlic and fry in oil until brown, then add the rice and fry for 3 minutes, stirring continuously. Remove the rice from the frypan and put in a saucepan with 3 cups of the reserved stock from the chicken. Cook slowly by the absorption method (p. 23) until ready.

Pound the ginger and chilli to a fine paste, add the black beans and pound a little more so as to break the beans into coarse pieces. Put mixture in a saucepan, add the remaining stock, and bring to the boil. Stir in the remaining sauce ingredients and simmer for 5 minutes. Taste and adjust if necessary — the sweet, salt and sour tastes should all be noticeable, with the sour slightly dominant.

Serve in individual portions, each having a mound of rice with the chicken placed carefully on top, the sauce spooned over it, and slices of cucumber and sprigs of coriander arranged around it. Serves four.

Light Meals – *Rice and Noodles*

KAO MOO DAENG

RICE AND RED PORK

4 cups freshly cooked rice (see p. 23)

Red pork:

500 g pork fillet
2 tablespoons light soy sauce
1 tablespoon hoi sin sauce OR tomato paste
1 tablespoon whisky
1 tablespoon sugar
400 mL water

Sauce:

$\frac{1}{2}$ tablespoon cornflour
1 tablespoon vinegar (to taste)

Garnishes:

3 small Lebanese cucumbers or fresh gherkins, sliced OR 1 small cucumber
20 sprigs coriander
3 large mild red and green chillies, cut into fine rings
3 tablespoons dark soy sauce
1 tablespoon vinegar

Cut the pork into long strips about 5 cm wide. Mix all the marinade ingredients (light soy sauce, hoi sin sauce, whisky, sugar and water) and work the pork well into the marinade. Leave to marinate for at least 1 hour — several hours would be better.

Preheat the oven to 200°C and bake the pork in its marinade for about 30 minutes, frequently spooning the marinade over it. Remove from the oven, take out the pork but save the remainder of the marinade. Grill the pork under your grill or broiler until the surface is dry and brown, then slice it into thin (5 mm wide) slices and set aside.

To make the sauce, dissolve the cornflour in the remaining marinade; add water to make up to 1 cup if there is less than that left. (If you have added much water a little more light soy sauce may be needed.)

Add the vinegar and adjust to taste. Simmer until the flour is cooked and the sauce thickens, then remove from the heat.

To serve, place about 1 cup of boiled rice on each plate. Arrange the pork pieces on top and spoon the sauce over it. Arrange cucumber slices and coriander sprigs around it. Mix the chillies with the soy sauce and vinegar, and serve in a separate bowl. Serves four.

KAO MUN

RICE COOKED IN COCONUT MILK

3 cups rice
4 cups thin coconut milk (see p. 7)

Wash the rice, put it in a saucepan and cook by the absorption method (see page 23), but using thin coconut milk instead of water. This quantity serves 6 — allow half a cup per person if cooking more or less.

Kao Mun is a more luxurious alternative to *Kao* (plain boiled rice, see p. 23); it would often be served with a small meal of only one or two dishes. A typical menu is given on p. 3.

Light Meals – *Rice and Noodles*

KAO PAD

FRIED RICE

1 tablespoon oil
100 g pork fillet, sliced into paper thin 2 cm × 2 cm squares
1 capsicum (bell pepper), diced into 1 cm squares
2 tablespoons nam pla (fish sauce)
2 tablespoons tomato sauce
4 spring onions, chopped into 5 mm lengths
3 cups cooked rice (see p. 23)

Garnish:

1 small cucumber, sliced
3 spring onions
1 lemon or lime, cut into wedges
Nam Pla Prik (spiced fish sauce, see p. 84)

Heat the oil in a wok, toss in the pork and fry until cooked and browned. Add the capsicum then the *nam pla* and tomato sauce, and continue stirring for about 1 minute, then add the spring onions and finally the rice. Mix thoroughly, and stir for 1–2 minutes until the rice is warmed through.

Serve in individual portions, each with slices of cucumber, a whole spring onion and a wedge of lime or lemon arranged around the rice. Separately, provide a small bowl of *Nam Pla Prik*. The quantity given here will make a light lunch for 2 to 3 people — it can be "stretched" if required by increasing the rice to 4 cups.

This recipe can be varied according to the ingredients available — in its simplest form only pork and thinly sliced onions would be included. Leftover cooked meat could be used. For a more substantial lunch a bowl of *gaeng chud* (clear soup) would often be eaten with *Kao Pad*.

KAO KLUK GAPI

FRIED RICE WITH SHRIMP PASTE

1 egg
2 tablespoons oil
1 small onion, finely sliced
2 cloves garlic, chopped
½ cup dried shrimps
1 tablespoon gapi (shrimp paste)
4 cups cooked rice (see p. 23)
3 spring onions, coarsely chopped
1 large coriander plant, coarsely chopped

Garnish:

1 small cucumber, peeled and sliced
Fresh pineapple (or green mango), cubed
Moo Wan (sweet pork, see p. 61)

Beat the egg; heat a pan or wok and cover the surface with 1 tablespoon of oil. Slowly pour in the egg while rotating the pan to cover the surface. Cook until brown on one side (about 2 minutes) then flip it to cook the other side. Remove the omelette from the pan, allow to cool and cut into fine strips.

Heat the remaining tablespoon of oil in the wok, throw in the onion and garlic and stir until soft. Add the dried shrimps (chopped roughly if large, whole if small), stir for 1 minute then add the *gapi* and mix in with the other ingredients in the pan. Stir in the rice and mix well. Finally, throw in the spring onions and coriander and stir all together.

Serve the rice on individual plates decorated with strips of omelette. Place cucumber and pineapple alongside, with a few pieces of *Moo Wan*. This quantity provides a lunch for 2 or 3 people.

KAO KLUK GAPI
(Fried rice with shrimp paste), opposite
with MOO WAN
(sweet pork), recipe page 61

KANOM JEEN NAM YA GAI
(Noodles with spicy chicken sauce), recipe page 28

Light Meals – Rice and Noodles

GWAYTIO NAM

RICE NOODLES

500 g rice noodle
½ tablespoon oil
2 cloves garlic, chopped
250 g beef (topside or rump), thinly sliced
6 cups water or stock
3 tablespoons nam pla (fish sauce)
1 tablespoon light soy sauce
2 sticks celery, sliced
3 spring onions, cut into 1 cm pieces
100 g bean sprouts
3 coriander plants

Garnish:

Coriander leaves
Prik Nam Som (chillies in vinegar, see p. 84)
Nam Jim (dipping chilli sauce, see p. 82)

Rice noodle is bought fresh as a big, rolled sheet and is available from any Chinese supermarket. It will keep in the refrigerator for about a week.

Cut the rice noodle into strips about 1 cm wide. Fry the garlic in the oil in a deep pan, then add the meat and brown quickly. Pour in the water or stock, add the *nam pla*, soy sauce and celery and simmer until the meat is cooked (5–10 minutes depending upon how thinly it is sliced). Add the spring onions, bean sprouts and coriander (reserving a few leaves for garnishing), then the noodles. Cook for a further 2 minutes, then serve — garnished perhaps with a few fresh coriander leaves.

This is a "wet" noodle dish — it would be served in a bowl but is much more substantial than a soup. You can serve it with *Prik Nam Som* or *Nam Jim*.

SEN MEE LAD NAH

NOODLES WITH FOOD OVER THEIR FACE

300 g sen mee (rice vermicelli)
2 tablespoons oil
2 tablespoons dark soy sauce
5 cloves garlic, chopped
300 g beef sirloin or rump, thinly sliced
450 g broccoli, cut into small pieces (including pieces of stalk, which should be peeled)
1 tablespoon oyster sauce
1 tablespoon nam pla (fish sauce)
1 tablespoon tapioca flour OR cornflour
200 mL water

Accompaniment:

1 large chilli, sliced
2 tablespoons vinegar

Rice vermicelli is a fine noodle made from rice flour. It is widely available from supermarkets and delicatessens as well as Asian shops.

Soak the vermicelli in warm water for 15 minutes. Heat 1 tablespoon of oil in a wok, drain the noodles and tip them in. Add the soy sauce and stir until the noodles are cooked — this should take about 2 minutes. Remove the noodles and put them aside. Heat the remaining tablespoon of oil and fry the garlic until golden, then add the meat and stir until brown. Add the broccoli, oyster sauce and *nam pla*, still stirring, then the flour mixed with the water. Stir until cooked (about 5 minutes — longer if the pieces of broccoli are a bit large).

To serve, place a helping of noodles on each plate then spoon the meat and broccoli "over its face". As an accompaniment serve the sliced chilli in vinegar in a small bowl. This quantity will serve 4 people, but it can easily be scaled up or down.

Light Meals – Rice and Noodles

KANOM JEEN NAM YA GAI

NOODLES WITH SPICY CHICKEN SAUCE

5 pieces dried krachai (lesser ginger)
2 cups water
1 stalk lemon grass, chopped into 2 cm pieces
2–3 red chillies, chopped and seeded
2 cloves garlic, peeled
$\frac{2}{3}$ small onion, chopped
500 g chicken fillet
$\frac{1}{2}$ cup thick coconut milk (see p. 7)
1 teaspoon palm or raw sugar
1 tablespoon nam pla (fish sauce)
350 g kanom jeen (somen) noodles

Accompaniment:

100 g green beans
200 g pak boong (swamp cabbage, see p. 11) OR spinach or silverbeet
The remainder of the chopped onion
1 tablespoon oil
150 g bean sprouts
2 hard-boiled eggs, quartered
30 basil leaves

Krachai, Lesser Ginger (Kaempferia pandurata) is a member of the ginger family, with a milder flavour than ginger. It is available in dried form from the larger Asian supermarkets or from any shop specialising in Thai food. Sometimes it is labelled rather uninformatively "Dried Rhizome" — in case of doubt it can be distinguished from ka (galingale) by the size and shape of the pieces. A packet of krachai will contain a mixture of small (less than 1 cm) slices and long thin strips, whereas dried ka comes in much larger slices.

Soak dried krachai, in just enough water to cover it, for 15 minutes before use. Of course, if you are lucky enough to have fresh krachai, you should use it instead, without soaking. Ka (galingale) could be used as a substitute at a pinch, but would change the flavour somewhat.

Kanom jeen are straight, white wheaten noodles like very thin vermicelli. They are most often seen in Asian shops under their Japanese name, "somen".

Put 2 cups of water in a large saucepan, add the soaked krachai, lemon grass, chillies, garlic, onion and chicken, and bring to the boil. Simmer for 10 minutes. Remove all the ingredients (except the chicken) from the liquid and blend in a liquidiser, adding a little of the liquid as required. Add half of the chicken to the blender and blend in with the paste. Shred the remaining chicken into strips. Bring the stock back to the boil, stir in the blended mixture and the coconut milk, and add the shredded chicken. Add the sugar and nam pla (to taste). Simmer for a further 10 minutes. Meanwhile, cook the noodles for about 5 minutes in boiling salted water and drain.

Cut the beans into 3–5 cm pieces; remove the stalks and old leaves from the pak boong or spinach and cut the leaves into strips. Lightly steam or boil the beans and the pak boong. Fry the remaining onion in the oil for 3 minutes.

To serve, place a helping of noodles in the middle of a plate, put a little fried onion with some of the oil it was fried in on top, then arrange small amounts of bean sprouts, green beans, pak boong and a quarter of an egg around the pile of noodles. Pour a generous ladle of sauce over the noodles and garnish with a few basil leaves. The quantity given here will serve 6 generously.

Light Meals – Rice and Noodles

SEN CHAN PAD KATI

FRIED RICE STICKS IN COCONUT SAUCE

200 g rice sticks
1 cup thick coconut milk } *(see p. 7)* *1 cup thin coconut milk*
OR *1 400 mL tin + 100 mL water*
2 cloves garlic, chopped
½ small onion, chopped
150 g pork fillet, cut into small thin slices, *about 1 cm × 2 cm and 2 mm thick*
2 tablespoons tinned yellow (soy) beans (see p. 10)
100 g bean curd (tofu), cut into 1 cm cubes
2 teaspoons palm or raw sugar
2 teaspoons nam pla (fish sauce)
1 teaspoon tamarind concentrate OR *2 tablespoons tamarind water (see p. 11)*
200 g bean sprouts
10 small Chinese chives, cut into 3 cm lengths

Accompaniments:

Lime, cut in wedges
Dried chillies, coarsely ground
Chinese chives
Bean sprouts
Coriander leaves

Rice "sticks" are a form of rice noodle which come as dried flattened sticks. When cooked they are like Italian fettucine in shape and texture.

Soak the rice sticks in warm water for 15 minutes then drain. Heat the thick and thin coconut milk in a wok and allow to boil gently for about 3 minutes. Add the garlic and onion and cook until soft, then add the pork and yellow beans and stir until the pork is cooked (5–10 minutes, depending on how thinly it is sliced). Add the bean curd, sugar, *nam pla* and tamarind, mix well and adjust the seasoning to taste. Throw in the bean sprouts and chives and cook for another 2 minutes. Tip out half of the sauce and set

aside. Add the rice sticks to the wok and cook for a further 5 minutes.

Serve on individual plates, pouring some of the reserved sauce over each serving. Scatter a few coriander leaves over each. Serve wedges of lime, whole Chinese chives, raw bean sprouts and a dish of coarsely ground dried chilli separately, for the guests to help themselves to. This quantity will serve 4.

SEN MEE PAD GAI

RICE VERMICELLI WITH CHICKEN

300 g sen mee (rice vermicelli)
3 coriander plants
1 tablespoon oil
3 cloves garlic, chopped
1 small onion, chopped
200 g chicken fillet, cut into small pieces *approximately 3 cm × 2 cm × 1 cm*
50 mL water
1 tablespoon sugar
2 tablespoons nam pla (fish sauce)
2 tablespoons tamarind water (see p. 11) OR *1 teaspoon tamarind concentrate*
5 spring onions, cut into 1 cm pieces

Soak the noodles in warm water until soft (around 15 minutes), then drain. Cut the coriander (stems and leaves) into 1 cm pieces, reserving the leaves of one coriander plant whole for use as garnish.

Heat the oil in a wok or pan, throw in the garlic, onion and chicken and fry until brown. Add the water, sugar, *nam pla* and tamarind and adjust to taste, then put in the coriander, spring onions and noodles and mix thoroughly until the noodles are cooked (about 5 minutes).

Garnish with the reserved coriander leaves when serving.

Light Meals – Rice and Noodles

MEE KROB

CRISPY NOODLES

125 g sen mee (rice vermicelli)
About 2 cups oil for deep-frying
75 g bean curd (tofu) cut into "matchsticks", 3 mm × 3 mm × 30 mm
1 clove garlic, chopped
1 small onion, chopped
200 g pork or chicken fillet, chopped finely
100 g green (raw) prawn meat, chopped finely
OR 200 g green prawns, peeled and chopped
1 tablespoon black beans (tinned)
2 tablespoons vinegar
2 tablespoons nam pla (fish sauce)
4 tablespoons palm or brown sugar
2 tablespoons lemon juice
2 dried chillies, pounded to a coarse powder

Accompaniments:

125 g bean sprouts
1 bunch Chinese chives
Lemon or lime wedges

Garnish:

1 head pickled garlic, sliced thinly
1 red chilli, sliced thinly
Coriander leaves

Put the bundle of rice vermicelli in a deep bowl (to prevent it flying everywhere) and break it up with your hands just enough for the noodles to separate freely. Heat the oil in a wok and fry the bean curd "matchsticks" until they are crisp and beginning to brown. Remove them with a slotted spoon and place on kitchen paper to drain. Making sure that the oil stays very hot, fry the noodles, a little at a time. They will puff up instantly they hit the hot oil, and should then be removed. Each batch will take no more than 15 seconds, and the quantity given here should be fried in four or five batches. It is important that the noodles all hit the oil at once, otherwise either some noodles will not puff up, or the rest of the batch will soak up too much oil while you try to make the last few "go". Stand the fried noodles on kitchen paper to drain. At this point the quantity will look positively enormous, but do not panic — they shrink when they are added to the sauce.

Pour out all of the oil except one tablespoon. Fry the garlic and onion over a high heat until they are beginning to brown, then add the pork or chicken and fry until it is cooked. This will only take a couple of minutes if you really did chop it finely. Add the chopped prawn and fry a minute more, then reduce the heat. Add the black beans, vinegar, nam pla, sugar and lemon juice. Stir well and allow to simmer for a few moments, then taste and adjust as necessary. Add the pounded chilli, to taste. (The chilli is only intended to give a little bit of "bite" and can be reduced or omitted if you prefer.) Still over a low heat, add the noodles and bean curd and mix everything together rapidly and thoroughly.

Serve immediately, or the noodles will become soggy, with the pickled garlic, sliced chilli and coriander leaves scattered on top and the bean sprouts and Chinese chives arranged around, and a wedge of lemon for each person. This quantity serves four people.

Pickled garlic is available at Asian supermarkets, but it can be omitted if you cannot find it (or if you don't like it). Spring onions or ordinary chives could be used in place of the Chinese chives.

<u>Soups</u>

Soups

In Thailand soups are served in separate bowls to each guest, but at the same time as the rice and all the other courses. You can eat the soup separately, or spoon it onto your plate and eat it with rice — the choice is yours, and neither would raise any eyebrows.

GAI TOM KA

CHICKEN SOUP WITH GALINGALE

2 pieces of fresh ka (galingale) each about 5 cm long OR 10 slices dried ka
3 cups thin coconut milk (see p. 7)
250 g chicken fillet, cut into 2 cm × 3 cm pieces
2 tablespoons nam pla (fish sauce) (to taste)
3 tablespoons lemon juice
5 small hot chillies (to taste)

Garnish:

1 coriander plant, finely chopped
2 spring onions, finely chopped

Wash and peel the ka, and cut it into slices 3 mm thick. Bring the coconut milk and chicken to the boil in a saucepan, add the ka, and simmer uncovered for 10–15 minutes. Add the nam pla and lemon juice (to taste), bruise the chillies with the side of a knife and add them, then cook for a further 2–3 minutes until the chicken is cooked.

Garnish the soup with the coriander and spring onions just before serving.

GAENG LEUANG

YELLOW CURRY SOUP

5 small dried chillies
2 cloves garlic, peeled
$\frac{1}{2}$ teaspoon powdered turmeric
$\frac{1}{2}$ small onion, peeled and chopped
1 stalk lemon grass, chopped
$\frac{1}{2}$ teaspoon salt
1 teaspoon gapi (shrimp paste)
One medium-sized fish (snapper, bream or perch)
3 cups water
250 g bamboo shoots
1 tablespoon nam pla (fish sauce)
2 tablespoons tamarind water (see p. 11) OR 1 teaspoon tamarind paste

Soak the dried chillies in water for about 15 minutes, until soft. In a mortar, pound the chillies, garlic, turmeric, onion, lemon grass and salt to a fine paste. Add the gapi and mix in well.

Clean and scale the fish then score it with closely spaced vertical cuts. Cut it into 4 to 6 pieces. In a saucepan, stir the paste into the water then bring to the boil. Add the bamboo shoots, nam pla and tamarind water, taste and adjust as necessary. The sharp taste of the tamarind should be quite noticeable. Finally add the fish chunks, bring back to the boil and simmer until the fish is cooked — 5–10 minutes, depending on the fish used.

Soups

GAENG SOM
SOUR SOUP

5 whole black peppercorns
1 large mild chilli OR 3 small hot chillies
1 small onion
1 teaspoon gapi (shrimp paste)
1 tablespoon tamarind pulp
3 cups water
300 g white fish fillet
2 large zucchinis (courgettes) OR ¼ medium-sized cabbage

Using a mortar and pestle, pound together the peppercorns, chilli and onion to a coarse paste, then add the *gapi* and pound to mix all together. The alternative quantities of chilli are NOT equivalent — the former will give a mild soup, the latter will be quite hot. Either is quite authentic; the choice depends or your taste, or those of your guests.

Prepare the tamarind water by adding a cup of boiling water to the tamarind pulp. Stir well and leave at least 5 minutes then strain into another container.

Bring the 3 cups of water to the boil in a saucepan, add the fish and cook for 3 minutes. Remove the fish, add to the paste in the mortar and pound lightly. If you wish, you could reserve some of the fish in larger pieces. Return the paste and fish to the water, bring back to the boil, add the zucchinis and reserved pieces of fish. Add tamarind water to taste — about 4 tablespoons would be a suitable starting point. The soup should have a noticeable sour, tangy flavour from the tamarind.

Many different vegetables can be used in this soup. Among the more common ones used in Thailand would be *pak kad kao* (Chinese cabbage) or *marum* (the baton-like fruit of the Horseradish Tree, *Moringa oleifera*, which is used as a vegetable). Other possible alternatives would be cauliflower, turnip or snake beans. Prawns (raw, peeled and de-veined) could be used instead of fish. This soup would normally be made with only one vegetable, but if made with several it would be called *gaeng som ruam mit* — literally, "*gaeng som* amongst friends". Often an omelette — *Kai Gio* (see p. 66) — would be served with a *gaeng som*.

GAENG CHUD NOR MAI
BAMBOO SHOOT SOUP

200 g belly pork
1 tablespoon oil
3 cloves garlic, crushed
2 cups water or stock
200 g (drained weight) bamboo shoots, thinly sliced
¼ teaspoon cracked peppercorns
½ tablespoon nam pla (fish sauce)
Garnish:
Coriander leaves

Remove the skin and cut the meat into chunks about 4 cm long (leaving the bones on or removing them, as you please). Heat the oil in a saucepan, fry the garlic for a minute, add the pork and fry until brown. Add the water, bring to the boil and simmer for 5 minutes. Add the bamboo shoots, pepper and *nam pla* and simmer for a further 10 minutes or until all is cooked. Garnish with coriander leaves and serve.

This soup could equally be made with chicken instead of pork — chop the chicken into chunks, complete with bone.

Soups

GAENG CHUD KAO PAUD KAB HED

CLEAR SOUP WITH CORN AND MUSHROOM

2 cloves garlic
5 coriander roots
6 peppercorns
2 spring onions
1 tablespoon oil
200 g stewing pork, finely sliced
1½ cups water
2 tablespoons nam pla (fish sauce)
1 200 g tin baby corn, drained OR fresh baby corn
50 g oyster mushrooms OR straw or button mushrooms

Garnish:
Coriander leaves

Using a mortar and pestle pound the garlic, washed coriander roots and peppercorns to a coarse paste. Cut the spring onions into pieces about 3 cm long, leave the baby corn and mushrooms whole unless they are very large. Heat the oil in a saucepan and fry the paste for half a minute, then throw in the pork and stir until browned. Add the water, bring to the boil and add the *nam pla*. Simmer for 10 minutes. Add the corn and mushrooms and continue simmering until all is cooked — no more than 5 minutes. Garnish with coriander leaves before serving.

In Thailand straw mushrooms would most often be used for this soup, but oyster mushrooms or ordinary buttom mushrooms are quite acceptable. Alternative vegetables which could be used with the same basic recipe include squash, marrows or zucchini (courgettes), Chinese cabbage and turnip.

GAENG CHUD WOON SEN

CLEAR SOUP WITH NOODLES

30 g mung bean vermicelli
8 dried Chinese mushrooms
1 tablespoon oil
4 cloves garlic, coarsely chopped
200 g pork, cut into chunky pieces, about 2 cm × 1 cm × 1 cm
4 cups stock or water
4 coriander roots, bruised with the back of a cleaver
4 tablespoons nam pla (fish sauce)
8 spring onions, cut into 2.5 cm lengths

Soak the vermicelli and the mushrooms in hot water for 5–10 minutes, then cut the mushrooms into 1 cm strips. Heat the oil in a saucepan, add the garlic and fry for 1 minute, then add the pork and fry until browned. Add the stock or water and the coriander roots and bring to the boil. Add the vermicelli and mushrooms, then the *nam pla* (adjusting to taste). Add the spring onions, simmer for about 5 minutes, and serve.

Soups

GAENG CHUD PAK KAD DONG
PICKLED CABBAGE SOUP

6 cloves garlic
10 coriander roots
20 peppercorns
2 tablespoons oil
400 g pork spare rib, cut into 4 cm pieces
1 litre water or stock
400 g pickled cabbage (tinned or fresh)
1–3 tablespoons nam pla (fish sauce)

In Thailand there are two kinds of pickled cabbage, the "sweet" kind, which has sugar added to the pickling brine, and the "salty" kind, which does not. The pickled cabbage available in tins is usually the salty kind, but sometimes it is possible to buy fresh pickled cabbage in plastic bags in Asian shops. The sweet sort would be best here.

Pound the garlic, coriander roots and peppercorns together to a coarse paste. Heat the oil in a saucepan, fry the paste for 1 minute then add the pork and fry until brown. Add the water or stock and bring to the boil, then add the pickled cabbage and season with nam pla to taste (this will naturally depend on the saltiness of your pickled cabbage). Simmer for 15 minutes, then serve.

GAENG LIANG
EVENING SOUP

10 peppercorns
1 small onion
4 tablespoons dried shrimps
2 teaspoons gapi (shrimp paste)
5 cups stock
500 g (1 bunch) pak boong (swamp cabbage) cut into sections, each with a leaf and part of the stalk
40 basil leaves (preferably maengluk, see p. 7)
Nam pla (fish sauce) to taste

Pound the peppercorns, onion and dried shrimps to a coarse paste. Add the gapi and pound in well. In a saucepan, stir the paste into the stock and bring to the boil. Add the pak boong and basil leaves, bring back to the boil and simmer until the pak boong is cooked. Taste and add nam pla if it is not salty enough (this will depend on how salty your stock was).

Other vegetables could be used singly or in combination — Chinese cabbage, white cabbage, broccoli, cauliflower, carrot, marrow.

Soups

TOM YAM GOONG
HOT PRAWN SOUP

500 g large to medium green (raw) prawns
2 stalks lemon grass
3 small hot (birdseye) chillies
6 cups water
4 large slices dried or fresh ka (galingale)
1–2 tablespoons nam pla (fish sauce)
½ cup lemon juice
1 teaspoon Nam Prik Pao (see p. 83) — optional
Garnish:
Coriander leaves

Peel and wash the prawns, slit them down the back and remove the black "vein" (actually the gut). Cut the lemon grass into 3 cm lengths and bruise with the side of a cleaver (dried lemon grass pieces can be used). Bruise the chillies in the same way, but leave them whole.

Bring the water to the boil in a saucepan, throw in the lemon grass and galingale, cover and simmer for 10 minutes. Add the prawns, chillies and 1 tablespoon of nam pla. The prawns will cook quickly — around 3 minutes. Pour in the lemon juice, taste and if necessary add more nam pla. At the last moment stir in the Nam Prik Pao, if desired.

Pour into a bowl and float some coriander leaves on it as a garnish.

For many tourists this ubiquitous soup will be an enduring memory of meals eaten in Thailand. Nothing could be more Thai — and nothing could be more simple. The degree of heat can be adjusted to individual tastes by varying the amount and type of chillies and the time at which they are added — the longer they are in the soup the hotter it will be. The lemon grass and galingale are there to flavour the stock, and are not eaten. The same goes for the chillies so far as most farangs are concerned!

PLA MUK YAT SAI
STUFFED SQUID SOUP

6 small squid (about 10 cm body length)
30 g peeled prawns (about 3 medium-sized prawns), finely chopped
50 g minced pork
3 coriander roots
1 clove garlic
5 peppercorns
1½ tablespoons nam pla (fish sauce)
100 mL water
1 coriander plant, cut into 3 cm pieces
3 spring onions, cut into 3 cm pieces

Clean the squid, but do not score or slice them. Cut off the tentacles and save them, and keep the body sac whole (but scraped until it is white). Mix the prawns with the minced pork. In a mortar, pound the coriander roots, garlic and peppercorns to a paste. Add the pork and prawn mixture, and continue pounding until all is amalgamated to a smooth paste. Add ½ tablespoon of nam pla, and mix in well.

Stuff this mixture into the squid sacs, leaving about a centimetre of space to allow the stuffing to expand. Put the stuffed squid, the tentacles, and the water in a saucepan with 1 tablespoon of nam pla. Bring to the boil, and simmer for 20 minutes. A few minutes before the end of cooking throw in the coriander and spring onion.

Although this has only a relatively small amount of liquid, it would still be served as a soup — that is, serve out in individual bowls for each guest. Naturally, you will have to allow one squid per person, and adjust the quantities accordingly. For an added touch of theatre, serve from a "Chinese steamboat" at the table.

Thai Curries
Gaeng

Thai Curries – *Gaeng*

The word *gaeng* literally means casserole or stew — anything with a lot of sauce or liquid — but it is usually translated into English as "curry", since all *gaengs* are hot. In fact, the only one that a Thai would call curry is *Gaeng garee* — the Thai version of an Indian-style curry. A *gaeng* of some type is an essential component of a Thai dinner — the assortment of dishes will vary, but one will always be a fiery curry cooked in coconut milk.

Making curry pastes

Many families in Thailand never make their own curry paste — they would buy them fresh from their favourite stall at the local market. Outside Thailand they can be bought at Asian shops; it is often easier to buy the ready-made paste than to get the ingredients. While some substitutions can be made — lime peel for *makrut*, for example — we would suggest buying paste rather than using inappropriate substitutes for half the ingredients.

Many European books on Asian food suggest using food processors, but no Thai ones do! We feel that a curry paste is too thick (or should be) to make such devices worthwhile. A coffee grinder (reserved for the purpose) could be handy for the dry spices, but once the moist ingredients are added a mortar and pestle is the easiest way — a traditional large, heavy, stone one from a Chinese store is best.

The recipes given make enough paste for around six curries. Stored in a closed jar in the fridge, curry pastes should keep for weeks. You can freeze them if you need to keep them longer than that. Some curries, such as *Gaeng Kuoa Sapparot* (see p. 47) have their own specific paste; for these the appropriate quantities for one curry are given in the recipe.

Almost all recipes requiring a curry paste contain the instruction "fry until it smells cooked". This means until it is bubbling and just beginning to brown, and giving off a strong curry smell; it only takes a minute or two (more if a lot of coconut milk must be reduced down before it starts to fry).

KREUNG GAENG KEO WAN

GREEN CURRY PASTE

6 large slices fresh or dried ka (galingale) OR *3 teaspoons powdered ka (laos powder)*
40 fresh small green (birdseye) chillies, finely chopped
4 stalks lemon grass, finely chopped
1 teaspoon makrut (Kaffir lime) rind (fresh or dried) OR *lime peel*
Roots of 2 coriander plants, finely chopped
2 teaspoons salt
½ teaspoon peppercorns (white for preference)
2 tablespoons coriander seeds
2 teaspoons cumin seeds
1 small onion, finely chopped
10 cloves garlic, finely chopped
2 teaspoons gapi (shrimp paste)

Soak the *ka* (if dried slices are used) in water for 15 minutes or so, until soft, then drain. Chop the *ka* as fine as you can. Put the chillies, *ka*, lemon grass, *makrut*, coriander roots and salt into a mortar and pound to a fine paste. Add the peppercorns and coriander and cumin seeds (pre-ground, if you like, in a coffee grinder), and pound until well blended. Add the onion and garlic and pound again to a fine paste. Finally, add the *gapi* and pound once more until all is mixed. Store, well covered, in the refrigerator until needed.

Thai Curries – Gaeng

KREUNG GAENG PED
RED CURRY PASTE

20 dried red chillies
4 large slices fresh or dried ka (galingale) OR 2 teaspoons powdered ka (laos powder)
2 stalks lemon grass, finely chopped
1 teaspoon makrut (Kaffir lime) rind (fresh or dried) OR lime peel
Roots of 2 coriander plants, finely chopped
2 teaspoons salt
$\frac{1}{2}$ teaspoon peppercorns (white for preference)
2 tablespoons coriander seeds
2 teaspoons cumin seeds
1 small onion, finely chopped
10 cloves garlic, finely chopped
2 teaspoons gapi (shrimp paste)

Soak the chillies (and *ka*, if dried slices are used) in water for 15 minutes or so, until soft, then drain. Chop them as finely as you can. Put the chillies, *ka*, lemon grass, *makrut*, coriander roots and salt into a mortar and pound to a fine paste. Add the peppercorns and coriander and cumin seeds (pre-ground, if you like, in a coffee grinder), and pound until well blended. Add the onion and garlic and pound again to a fine paste. Finally, add the *gapi* and pound once more until all is mixed. Store, well covered, in the refrigerator until needed.

Gaeng ped literally means "hot curry" but is always translated into English as "red curry". It is made with dried red chillies, while *gaeng keo wan* (literally "green sweet curry") is always made with *fresh* green chillies.

KREUNG GAENG MASAMAN
MUSLIM CURRY PASTE

1 small onion
12 cloves garlic
2 teaspoons gapi (shrimp paste)
4 slices fresh or dried ka (galingale)
8 dried chillies
4 stalks lemon grass, chopped finely
$\frac{1}{2}$ teaspoon peppercorns
2 tablespoons coriander seeds
2 tablespoons cumin seeds
6 cloves

Peel and quarter the onion, peel the garlic then wrap them together in aluminium foil and roast in the ash of a charcoal barbecue for 15 minutes. Wrap the *gapi* separately and roast it in the same way. (Traditionally, banana leaves should be used — try it if you have a banana tree in your garden.) Chop the *ka* (galingale) finely, and throw it with all the other ingredients into a dry wok and shake over a moderate heat for 5 minutes or so, until they begin to turn brown. In a mortar, pound all the ingredients, except the *gapi*, together to a smooth paste. Add the *gapi*, and pound again until mixed. Store, covered, in the refrigerator until needed.

The traditional Thai stove is an earthenware pot called *tao than*, containing smouldering charcoal. Raised castellations at the top support a wok or a grill as required. The ashes at the bottom are an ideal place for roasting the spices for this paste. Failing this, any shape or size of barbecue will do, or the ashes of an open fireplace in winter.

PANANG NEUEA
(Meatballs with peanut sauce), recipe page 61

NEUEA KEM
(Dried salty beef), recipe page 60
GAENG KEO WAN GAI
(Green chicken curry), recipe page 45

Thai Curries — *Gaeng*

PONG GAREE
CURRY POWDER

2 teaspoons fenugreek
2 teaspoons turmeric
1 teaspoon coriander
1 teaspoon cumin
¼ teaspoon peppercorns
1 cardamon pod (chopped)
Pinch each of:
dried ginger
cinnamon
cloves
nutmeg

The spices may be whole or ground. Grind the whole ones together to a fine powder in a mortar and pestle or coffee (or spice) grinder. Add the powdered ones, and mix well.

Many Thai recipes call for curry powder (see *Gaeng Garee Gai*, p. 46, *Sateh*, p. 15, and *Gai Pad Pong Garee*, p. 58). Any mild, aromatic one will do — there is no point in using a hot curry powder since you will make the dish as hot as you require with chilli. If you cannot find one you like, or wish to make everything yourself, try this recipe. It contains no chilli, so will add no heat to the dish itself. If you are using it in a European recipe which requires curry powder, add powdered chilli as well to taste.

GAENG KEO WAN MOO
GREEN CURRY OF PORK

500 g lean stewing pork, sliced into thin strips
2 cups thin coconut milk (see p. 7)
1 tablespoon green curry paste (Kreung Gaeng Keo Wan, see p. 41)
1 cup thick coconut milk (see p. 7)
30 fresh basil leaves OR 2 tablespoons dried basil
3–4 makrut (Kaffir lime) or lemon leaves
2 teaspoons nam pla (fish sauce)
100 g makeua pooang (pea eggplants) — optional
1–2 fresh green chillies, cut into long thin strips

Makeua pooang are tiny pea-sized eggplants (aubergines), which are crunchy and slightly bitter. If they are not available there is little point in trying to substitute anything else; the dish is more authentic · with no added vegetables than with inappropriate ones!

Simmer the pork in the thin coconut milk for 20–30 minutes in an uncovered pan. Remove the pork from the pan, pour out the coconut milk and set aside. Mix the curry paste with 2 tablespoons from the thick coconut milk and boil vigorously until the oil comes out from the milk and the paste starts to fry; fry for 2 minutes until it smells cooked (see p. 41). Throw in the meat and fry for a further 2 minutes. Reduce the heat and return the thin coconut milk to the pan. Bring back to the boil and add the torn basil and *makrut* (or lemon) leaves and the *nam pla*. Add the *makeua pooang*. Simmer another 5 minutes then add the remainder of the thick coconut milk. Simmer a further 15 minutes. Just before the end of cooking add the green chillies.

It is important always to keep the pan uncovered and to stir from time to time, or the coconut milk will curdle.

A green curry of beef (*Gaeng Keo Wan Neuea*) is made in exactly the same way, but substituting lean beef for the pork.

Thai Curries – Gaeng

GAENG PED GAI
RED CURRY OF CHICKEN

500 g chicken fillet
1 cup thick coconut milk ⎫ (see p. 7) 1 cup thin coconut milk ⎭ OR 1 400 mL tin + 200 mL water
1 tablespoon red curry paste (Kreung Gaeng Ped, see p. 42)
6 makrut (Kaffir lime) or lemon leaves
30 basil leaves OR 2 tablespoons dried basil
1 tablespoon nam pla (fish sauce)
1 fresh red chilli, cut in slivers
Garnish:
Fresh basil leaves

Cut the chicken into bite-sized pieces (3 cm × 2 cm). Put ¼ cup of the thick coconut milk into a saucepan and stir in the curry paste. Cook until the oil comes out and the paste smells cooked (about 2 minutes), then throw in the chicken and fry for a further 2−3 minutes, stirring constantly. Add the thin coconut milk, the (torn) *makrut* and basil leaves and the *nam pla*. Simmer for 10−15 minutes, then add the remaining thick coconut milk and the chilli. Simmer for a further 5 minutes then serve, with a few basil leaves thrown on top as a garnish.

A *gaeng* reheats well, and if you are preparing a complex meal you can make it in advance and reheat before serving. *Never* cover the pan while cooking or reheating.

GAENG PED GOONG
RED CURRY OF PRAWNS

1 cup thick coconut milk ⎫ (see p. 7) 1 cup thin coconut milk ⎭ OR 1 400 mL tin + 200 mL water
1 tablespoon red curry paste (Kreung Gaeng Ped, see p. 42)
6 makrut (Kaffir lime) or lemon leaves
30 basil leaves OR 2 tablespoons dried basil
1 tablespoon nam pla (fish sauce)
700 g green (raw) prawns, peeled and de-veined (see p. 36) OR 500 g peeled green prawns, de-veined
1 fresh red chilli, cut in slivers
Garnish:
Fresh basil leaves

Put ¼ of the cup of the thick coconut milk into a saucepan and stir in the curry paste. Cook until the oil comes out and the paste smells cooked (about 2 minutes), then add the thin coconut milk, the torn *makrut* and basil leaves and the *nam pla*. Simmer (uncovered) for 10 minutes, then add the prawns, the remaining thick coconut milk and the chilli. Simmer for a further 5 minutes then serve, with a few fresh basil leaves thrown on top as a garnish.

GAENG PED NEUEA (MOO)
RED CURRY OF BEEF (PORK)

To make a red curry of beef or pork, follow the recipe for *Gaeng Keo Wan Moo* (green curry of pork) on p. 43, substituting red curry paste for the green, and red chillies for the green ones, and omitting the *makeua pooang* (pea eggplants).

Thai Curries – Gaeng

GAENG KEO WAN TAOHU GUP SAI BUA

GREEN CURRY OF BEAN CURD WITH LOTUS STEM

300 g packet fresh bean curd (tofu)
500 g tin lotus "root" OR 300 g fresh lotus stem OR 500 g tin bamboo shoots
1 tablespoon green curry paste (Kreung Gaeng Keo Wan, see p. 41)
200 mL thick coconut milk 400 mL thin coconut milk } (see p. 7) OR 1 400 mL tin + 200 mL water
5 makrut (Kaffir lime) or lemon or lime leaves
20 basil leaves OR 1 tablespoon dried basil
1 tablespoon nam pla (fish sauce)
1 green chilli
Garnish:
Coriander leaves

Fresh lotus stem is 2–3 cm in diameter, and comes in long coils. The tinned lotus "root" (which anatomically seems also to be stem) is generally about twice that thickness, but both have a characteristic symmetrical pattern of air-spaces which is visually most attractive. If you cannot get lotus, bamboo shoots provide an alternative crisp vegetable to complement the soft bean curd. If you wish to make this curry strictly vegetarian, substitute light soy sauce for the *nam pla*, and use *tua nao* (bean paste) instead of *gapi* in the curry paste. (*Tua nao* is more often found in Asian food shops under its Vietnamese name, "*nuoc tuong hot*".)

Cut the tofu into 2 cm cubes; cut the lotus root or bamboo shoots into 3 mm thick slices. (If you have fresh lotus stem, peel it first and cut it into chunks about 3 cm long.) Mix the curry paste with 2 tablespoons of the thick coconut milk. Cook until the paste starts to fry; fry for 2 minutes until it smells cooked (see p. 41). Stir in the remaining coconut milk (thick and thin) and add the (torn) citrus and basil leaves and the *nam pla*. Add the tofu and lotus (or bamboo shoots), and simmer uncovered for 20–30 minutes until the lotus is softening but still crisp. Add the green chilli, cut in slivers, and simmer for 2 more minutes.

Scatter a few sprigs of coriander over the surface before serving.

GAENG KEO WAN GAI

GREEN CHICKEN CURRY

Make as *Gaeng Ped Gai* (red curry of chicken, p. 44), but use green curry paste, and green chillies instead of the red ones.

Thai Curries — *Gaeng*

GAENG MASAMAN NEUEA
MUSLIM BEEF CURRY

500 g chuck steak or similar, cut into 2 cm cubes
2 cups thin coconut milk ⎫ (see p. 7)
1 cup thick coconut milk ⎭
1 tablespoon Muslim curry paste (Kreung Gaeng Masaman, see p. 42)
1 medium potato (optional), cut into 2 cm chunks
1 small onion, cut into segments
50 g (3 tablespoons) raw peanuts, skinned
1 teaspoon cardamon pods
1 tablespoon lemon juice
3 tablespoons tamarind water (see p. 11)
1 tablespoon nam pla (fish sauce)
1 red chilli, sliced lengthways and seeded

Put the meat and the thin coconut milk into a pan, bring to the boil and simmer for 20 minutes. Remove the meat and pour out the coconut milk, leaving 4 tablespoons in the pan. Stir in the curry paste, and cook until the paste smells cooked — that is, it gives off a strong curry fragrance. Return the meat to the pan, and toss it in the paste and fry for a further 3–4 minutes. Pour the remainder of the thin coconut milk back in, and simmer for a further 10 minutes, until the sauce thickens and the oil separates and forms a layer on the surface. Add the potato, onion, peanuts, cardamon, lemon juice, tamarind water, *nam pla* and the thick coconut milk. Simmer for a further 30 minutes or until the meat and vegetables are cooked. Taste and adjust the seasoning with *nam pla*, lemon juice or tamarind as necessary. A few minutes before serving, add the chilli.

This *gaeng* is popular with Thai Muslims, and they generally would not eat the other varieties of Thai curry. Buddhist (and Christian) Thais are not so fussy, and eat *Gaeng Masaman* as well as the rest. Naturally, this is one dish in which one would *not* substitute pork for beef.

GAENG GAREE GAI
YELLOW CHICKEN CURRY

750 g chicken, with bone
1 tablespoon red curry paste (Kreung Gaeng Ped, see p. 42)
2 teaspoons curry powder (Pong Garee, see p. 43)
1 cup thick coconut milk ⎫ (see p. 7)
2 cups thin coconut milk ⎭
1 large potato (or 2 small), peeled and cut into 3 cm × 5 cm chunks
1 medium onion, peeled and quartered
1 tablespoon nam pla (fish sauce)
1 chilli (yellow-orange for preference), quartered and seeded

Accompaniment:

Ah Jahd (pickled cucumber, see p. 16)

Chop the chicken into largish pieces (drumsticks, for example, would be left whole). In a heavy pan, mix the curry paste and powder with 2 tablespoons of the thick coconut milk. Heat until the spices are frying and cook for around 2 minutes, until they smell cooked. Add the chicken pieces, and fry for 2–3 minutes, tossing them around so that they become coated with the curry mixture. Tip in the remaining thick coconut milk, and the thin coconut milk. Add the potato, onion and the *nam pla*. Simmer uncovered for about 30 minutes, until the meat and vegetables are cooked. Just before serving, add the chilli.

A side-dish of *Ah Jahd* would normally be served with this curry.

A vegetarian *Gaeng Garee* could be made using additional vegetables (cauliflower and carrot, for example) in place of the chicken.

Thai Curries — Gaeng

GAENG PAA
WILD CURRY

1 small eggplant (aubergine)
1 tablespoon oil
½ tablespoon red curry paste *(Kreung Gaeng Ped, see p. 42)*
250 g beef, sliced into thin strips
1 cup water
½ tablespoon nam pla (fish sauce)
150 g (drained weight) bamboo shoots, sliced
1 small capsicum (green pepper), *cut into bite-size pieces*
1 large red chilli, quartered and seeded
2 sticks fresh peppercorns OR *1 teaspoon drained green peppercorns*
20 leaves basil

Cut the eggplant into wedges and sprinkle with salt. Leave for 30 minutes, then wash well and blot dry. Fry the curry paste in the oil until it smells cooked (2–3 minutes), then throw in the meat and continue frying. Add the water, bring to the boil and simmer for 15 minutes. Add the *nam pla* (to taste), bamboo shoots, eggplant, capsicum, chilli, peppercorns and basil (reserving some leaves for garnish). Simmer for 2–3 minutes longer, until the vegetables are cooked. Garnish with fresh basil leaves and more chillies.

A "wild curry" is the type of curry that in Thailand would be used to cook game. This would most commonly be wild boar, and boar or venison would go very well with this recipe — increase the length of simmer if the meat is tough.

Fresh peppercorns are always used in this dish in Thailand; they are not even removed from their stalks — the whole string or bunch (about 5 cm long) is put in. It is not easy to buy fresh peppercorns outside tropical regions, though there seems to be no reason why they could not be imported into cooler climates — they must be easier to transport than most tropical fruits. Tinned green peppercorns, which can be bought in any supermarket, are the best substitute.

GAENG KUOA SAPPAROT
PRAWN AND PINEAPPLE CURRY

Curry paste:
3 dried chillies
3 tablespoons dried shrimps, pounded
3 stalks lemon grass
5 cm piece ka (galingale) OR *2 teaspoons dried or powdered ka*
½ small onion
¼ teaspoon salt
½ teaspoon gapi (shrimp paste)
Curry:
300 g green (raw) prawns, *peeled and de-veined (see p. 36)*
½ small pineapple, peeled and *cut into 2 cm × 3 cm × 1 cm pieces*
400 mL thick coconut milk (see p. 7)
1 teaspoon palm or raw sugar
1 tablespoon nam pla (fish sauce)

Soak the chillies (and *ka*, if dried slices are used) in water until soft. Pound the shrimps to a powder and set aside. Finely chop up the lemon grass, *ka* and onion. Pound the chillies to a fine pulp with the salt, add the lemon grass and *ka* and continue pounding, then add the onion and pound to a fine paste. Add the *gapi*, mix in thoroughly, then finally add the dried shrimps and mix in.

Fry the paste in about 100 mL of the coconut milk for about 3 minutes, then add the remaining coconut milk and bring gently to the boil. Add the pineapple, sugar and *nam pla*, and adjust to taste. Finally, add the prawns and continue simmering, uncovered, until they are cooked (about 3 minutes).

Thai Curries – Gaeng

CHOO CHI PLA

FISH CURRY

1½ tablespoons red curry paste (Kreung Gaeng Ped, see p. 42)
200 mL thick coconut milk ⎱ (see p.7) 400 mL thin coconut milk ⎰ OR 1 400 mL tin coconut milk + 200 mL water
500 g whole small mackerel (pla thu or yellowtail), cleaned and gutted OR 500 g fillets of firm-fleshed fish
1 tablespoon sugar
1 tablespoon nam pla (fish sauce)
Garnish:
4 fresh makrut (Kaffir lime) or lime/lemon leaves, finely sliced

The Thai name of this dish is almost untranslatable (and slightly vulgar) — the best English approximation we can come up with is "Stinking Hot Fish"!

Mix the curry paste with 100 mL of the thick coconut milk and fry it until it smells cooked (see p. 41). Add the rest of the coconut milk (thick and thin, or the remainder of the tin plus the water) and bring to the boil. Add the fish, sugar and *nam pla* and simmer until the fish is cooked. Taste and add more *nam pla* if necessary. Serve garnished with *makrut* or lemon leaves.

Fish and Seafood Dishes

Fish and Seafood Dishes

PLA PRIO WAN
SWEET AND SOUR FISH

1 whole fish (snapper, bream, coral trout or parrotfish) (about 750 g–1 kg)
2 tablespoons nam pla (fish sauce)
Cooking oil

Sauce:

2 tablespoons oil
2 cloves garlic, finely chopped
4 tablespoons brown sugar
2 tablespoons vinegar
2 tablespoons nam pla (fish sauce)
1 piece ginger (about 2 cm long), finely chopped
1 large tomato, chopped
1 medium green capsicum (bell pepper), chopped
1 large or 2 small carrots, peeled and thinly sliced
$\frac{3}{4}$ cup water
1 medium chilli, cut into slivers

Garnish:

Coriander leaves

The fish must be cleaned and scaled. Make about six vertical cuts on each side, down to the bone, and rub in the *nam pla*. If time permits, allow to marinate for up to 1 hour. Traditionally, the fish is deep-fried in a wok. Heat enough oil to cover one side of the fish and fry it in hot oil, so that the skin crisps nicely, turning once. Your fish must fit your wok! We often prefer to rub the fish with a little oil and grill it, again turning once. In Thailand, one might equally well cook the fish over charcoal on a *tao tahn*.

If you have deep-fried the fish, pour out the oil, leaving 2 tablespoons in the wok. Otherwise, heat 2 tablespoons in the wok. Fry the garlic until it begins to brown. Reduce the heat and add the sugar. As soon as the sugar has all melted, and before it can burn, add the vinegar. Add the *nam pla*, ginger, tomato, capsicum and carrot, and cook, stirring constantly, until the vegetables begin to soften. Add the water and chilli, stir in well and bring back to the boil. Taste, and adjust the flavour if necessary by adding more sugar, *nam pla* or vinegar so that the sweet, sour and salty flavours blend harmoniously. Simmer for 1–2 minutes.

Arrange the fish on a large serving dish, pour the sauce over it and garnish with coriander leaves.

PLA RAD SAUS PRIK
FISH IN CHILLI SAUCE

Oil for deep-frying
2 tablespoons flour
400 g fish fillet (without skin), cut into 5 cm x 5 cm x 1 cm pieces
1 tablespoon nam pla (fish sauce)
2 tablespoons brown sugar
2 tablespoons Nam Prik Siracha (Siracha chilli sauce, see p. 84)

Garnish:

Coriander leaves

Heat the oil in a pan or wok, dust the pieces of fish with flour, and fry them until golden brown. Remove the fish and leave to drain on paper towels. Pour the oil out of the pan, leaving about 1 tablespoonful. Reheat this and add the *nam pla*, sugar and chilli sauce. Stir together and adjust to taste; the sugar should not completely overpower the sharpness of the chilli sauce.

Arrange the fish pieces on a dish and pour the sauce over them. Garnish with coriander leaves.

Fish and Seafood Dishes

PLA SAM ROT

THREE-FLAVOURED FISH

1 whole fish (bream, snapper, coral trout or parrotfish), about 750 g–1 kg
5 tablespoons nam pla (fish sauce)
1–3 red chillies
½ teaspoon salt
1 piece ka (galingale), 2–3 cm
10 small or 5 large coriander roots
10 peppercorns
5 cloves garlic
½ medium onion
2 tablespoons oil
4 tablespoons water
3 teaspoons sugar
4 tablespoons tamarind water (see p. 11) OR 2 teaspoons tamarind concentrate
5 spring onions, cut into 2–3 cm pieces

Garnish:

Coriander leaves
Red chilli, cut into fine slivers

The fish must be cleaned and scaled. Make about six vertical cuts on each side, down to the bone, rub in 3 tablespoons of the *nam pla* and marinate for up to 1 hour. Depending on its size and your facilities, either deep-fry the fish in a wok or rub it with a little oil and grill it, turning once (see *Pla Prio Wan*, p. 51).

In a mortar, pound the chillies (without seeds), salt, *ka*, coriander roots, peppercorns, garlic and onion to a coarse paste. Heat the oil in a wok or pan and fry the paste for 2 minutes, then add the water, the remaining 2 tablespoons of the *nam pla*, the sugar and the tamarind. Taste and adjust as necessary — it should be sour, sweet and salty. Add the spring onions; when they are soft (about 5 minutes) pour the sauce over the fish.

Serve garnished with coriander leaves and thin slivers of red chilli.

PLA PAD KUN CHAI

FRIED FISH AND CELERY

1 tablespoon oil
2 cloves garlic, chopped
2 sticks celery, cut into 2 cm pieces
½ tablespoon green (fresh) ginger (a piece about 5 cm long), cut into fine slivers
300 g fish fillet, cut into 5 cm x 5 cm x 2 cm pieces
1 tablespoon tinned yellow (soy) beans (see p. 10)

Heat the oil in a pan or wok and fry the garlic until soft. Add the celery, ginger, fish and yellow beans and cook for about 3 minutes until the fish is cooked.

Thai celery is much smaller than the European variety — little larger than parsley — and the leaves are used as well. Either is quite suitable for this dish. Take care if using the leaves of European celery — the green (outer) leaves of some varieties are very bitter (and a potent purgative). Taste them — if they are not bitter it is quite all right to include them.

GOONG PAD PAK

PRAWNS WITH VEGETABLES

½ tablespoon oil
1 clove garlic, chopped
200 g peeled raw prawns, de-veined (see p. 36) OR 400 g whole prawns, peeled and de-veined (see p. 36)
100 g mushrooms, sliced
100 g Chinese cabbage (Chinese leaves), washed and sliced
1 tablespoon water
1 tablespoon nam pla (fish sauce)
1 coriander plant, chopped into short pieces

Heat the oil in a pan or wok and fry the garlic until golden. Add the prawns, mushrooms, Chinese cabbage and water and stir-fry over a high heat for 2–3 minutes. Add the *nam pla* and coriander, reduce the heat, stir for 1–2 minutes and serve.

Fish and Seafood Dishes

GOONG PAD KA

PRAWNS WITH GALINGALE AND PALM SUGAR

1 piece ka (galingale) about 5 cm long OR 1 piece green (fresh) ginger about 2 cm long
1 tablespoon oil
1 tablespoon palm sugar (or brown sugar, or honey)
1 teaspoon nam pla (fish sauce) OR light soy sauce
500 g green (raw) prawns, peeled and de-veined (see p. 36)

Garnish:

Lettuce leaves, chopped
Coriander leaves

Chop the *ka* or ginger finely; heat the oil in a wok and fry the *ka* until it just begins to brown. Lower the heat and add the sugar, and stir until it is all melted. Add the *nam pla* or soy sauce, then increase the heat and add the prawns. Stir continually until cooked (about 5 minutes).

Serve on a bed of chopped lettuce and garnish with coriander leaves.

Fresh ginger would definitely be a better bet for this dish than dried *ka*. In this case it would be called *Goong Pad King*.

HOY KLANG PAO

BARBECUED COCKLES

1 kg cockles
½ cup Nam Jim (dipping chilli sauce, see p. 82)
2 tablespoons raw peanuts, lightly crushed OR crunchy peanut butter
1 tablespoon coriander (stems and leaves), finely chopped

Wash and scrub the cockles in cold water. Throw them on the grill of a barbecue which is glowing nicely. Take them off as they open; this is all the cooking they need. As you eat them, dip each one in sauce made by adding peanuts and coriander to the *Nam Jim*.

Nam Jim is easy enough to make but it can also be bought in any Asian supermarket — look for a Thai chilli sauce with seeds in it. The Thai writing will certainly say *nam jim*, but what the English translation will be is rather less certain! It might say "coarse chilli sauce" or just "chilli sauce", or even "chicken chilli sauce" — the last name referring to the fact that it is eaten with roast or barbecued chicken throughout Thailand.

Fish and Seafood Dishes

PLA MUK PAD PRIK YUOK

SQUID WITH CAPSICUM

200 g cleaned squid
1 tablespoon oil for frying
2 cloves garlic, chopped
3 tablespoons water
1 tablespoon nam pla (fish sauce)
1 tablespoon palm or brown sugar
1 large green capsicum (bell pepper), cut into 3 cm x 3 cm pieces
1 tablespoon Nam Prik Siracha (Siracha chilli sauce, see p. 84) OR any sweet and mildish chilli sauce

Score the squid tubes all over in a crisscross pattern, then cut them into pieces about 2 cm x 3 cm. (If you start with whole squid you must first remove the eyes and the papery bone, and scrape the body-tube until it is white. Chop the tentacles and use them too.) The scoring is essential if the squid is to cook quickly and not become tough.

Heat the oil in a wok or frying pan, fry the garlic for 1 minute, stirring, then add the squid, still stirring, and the water. Add the *nam pla* and the sugar, and stir-fry for 2–3 minutes, until the squid is nearly cooked. Add the capsicum and chilli sauce and stir-fry for another 2–3 minutes.

TUA LUNTAO PAD PLA MUK

SNOW PEAS (MANGETOUT) WITH SQUID

200 g cleaned squid
200 g snow peas (mangetout)
1 tablespoon oil for frying
2 cloves garlic, chopped
3 tablespoons water
1 tablespoon nam pla (fish sauce)

Prepare the squid as in *Pla Muk Pad Prik Yuok* (see p. 53). Top and tail the snow peas and wash them. Heat the oil in a wok or frying pan, fry the garlic for 1 minute, stirring, then add the squid, still stirring, and the water. Add the *nam pla* and stir-fry for 2–3 minutes, until the squid is nearly cooked. Add the snow peas and stir-fry for another 2–3 minutes.

Meat and Poultry Dishes

Meat and Poultry Dishes

PANANG GAI

CHICKEN IN PEANUT SAUCE

1 clove garlic, finely chopped
Oil for frying
400 g chicken fillet, cut into thin strips
1 tablespoon red curry paste (Kreung Gaeng Ped, see p. 42)
200 mL thick coconut milk (see p. 7)
2 tablespoons peanuts, crushed OR crunchy peanut butter
Nam pla (fish sauce) to season

Garnish:

Coriander leaves
Red chillies, thinly sliced

Fry the garlic in a little oil until golden. Add the chicken and fry quickly for 1–2 minutes. Remove the chicken and fry the curry paste in the same oil for 1–2 minutes. Take the pan off the heat, stir in the coconut milk and the peanut butter. (Whole peanut kernels, pounded coarsely in a mortar and pestle, are best, but peanut butter, particularly the freshly made sort you can buy from health food shops, is quite acceptable.) Add the chicken, with a dash or two of *nam pla* to taste, and simmer for 15–20 minutes until the chicken is cooked. The sauce should be quite thick — much thicker than the sauce of a *gaeng* (curry).

Garnish with coriander leaves and red chillies.

GAI SAWAN

HEAVENLY CHICKEN

500 g chicken fillet, cut into 3 cm x 2 cm strips
Nam pla (fish sauce) to season
9–10 whole coriander roots (the roots of two bunches of coriander), washed
2 teaspoons black peppercorns
5 cloves garlic
Oil for frying

Garnish:

Coriander leaves

Sprinkle the chicken with a few drops of *nam pla* and set it aside while you prepare the paste. Using a mortar and pestle pound the coriander roots, peppercorns and garlic to a paste. In a bowl, stir the paste all around the chicken, so that it is thoroughly coated, and leave to marinate for at least 30 minutes. Heat 2–3 cm of oil in a wok and fry the chicken rather fast so that it cooks and browns without losing its juices and becoming soggy.

Garnish with some fresh coriander leaves.

The mixture of pepper, coriander root and garlic is called *sawan* (heavenly) in Thailand and is regarded as one of the basic flavours in cooking; it probably antedates the introduction of the now ubiquitous chilli in the sixteenth century.

Meat and Poultry Dishes

GAI PAD BAI GAPROW

CHICKEN WITH HOT BASIL

1 tablespoon oil
2 cloves garlic, chopped
300 g lean chicken mince
1 tablespoon dark soy sauce
2 tablespoons nam pla (fish sauce)
½ tablespoon brown sugar
60 gaprow (hot basil) leaves
5 small hot chillies, lightly crushed

Heat the oil in a pan or wok, fry the garlic for 1 minute then add the chicken mince and fry for a further 2 minutes. Add the soy sauce, *nam pla* and sugar, and mix thoroughly. Add the *gaprow* leaves (whole), and the chillies. Fry, stirring, until the chicken is cooked (about 5 minutes).

GAI PAD PONG GAREE

CHICKEN FRIED WITH CURRY POWDER

2 tablespoons oil
1 medium onion, diced
1 tablespoon curry powder (Pong Garee, see p. 43)
½ teaspoon ground coriander
250 g chicken fillet, diced
1 large potato, parboiled (about 15 minutes) and diced
½ cup chicken stock or water
½ teaspoon salt
½ teaspoon sugar

Heat the oil in a wok or frypan, fry the onion with the curry powder and coriander until soft but not brown, then add the chicken and potato and fry for a further 2 minutes. Add the stock or water with the salt and sugar and simmer until the liquid is reduced to half its original volume.

GAI PAD KING

CHICKEN WITH GINGER

4 dried Chinese mushrooms
1 tablespoon oil
1 clove garlic, coarsely chopped
300 g chicken fillet, cut into small strips
2–3 cm piece fresh (green) ginger, finely chopped
1 chilli, finely chopped
2 spring onions, cut into 1–2 cm pieces
1 tablespoon palm (or raw) sugar
2 tablespoons vinegar
1½ tablespoons nam pla (fish sauce)
½ cup water

Garnish:

Coriander leaves

Soak the dried mushrooms for 10 minutes in water that has just boiled, then cut them into strips 1 cm wide. Heat the oil in a wok or frypan and fry the garlic for 1–2 minutes, until golden. Add the chicken and fry, keeping the heat high, for 5 minutes or until cooked. Toss in the ginger, chilli, spring onions and mushrooms, and stir-fry for another 2 minutes. Add the sugar, stir it in well then add the vinegar and *nam pla*. Mix well then add the water. Bring to the boil, taste and adjust seasonings if necessary. Garnish with coriander leaves and serve.

GAI PAD BAI GAPROW
(Chicken with hot basil), recipe page 58
NAM PLA PRIK
(Spiced fish sauce), recipe page 84

PLA PRIO WAN
(Sweet and sour fish), recipe page 51

Meat and Poultry Dishes

LAAP NEUEA

ISSAN-STYLE STEAK TARTARE

⅓ cup rice
15 dried small red chillies (hot)
40 mint leaves
500 g best quality minced topside or rump
Juice of 3 lemons
1 small onion, finely chopped
5 stems of lemon grass, very finely chopped
Nam pla (fish sauce) to taste

Garnish:

Lettuce leaves
Red chillies, cut into slivers
Fresh salad vegetables

First roast the rice and the dried chillies in a dry frypan over a low heat, shaking or stirring continually, until the rice is opaque and brown (about 5 minutes). Using a mortar and pestle pound the rice and chillies to a sandy consistency. (You could possibly use a coffee grinder if you wished to minimise effort.) Chop the mint leaves finely, reserving a few whole mint leaves for garnishing. Mix the meat with the lemon juice, onion, mint and lemon grass and season with a dash or two of *nam pla*. Add the pounded rice and chilli, and mix in well. Taste — it should be quite sharp and hot — add more lemon juice if necessary.

Garnish with mint leaves and slivers of fresh red chillies, and serve on a bed of lettuce leaves, with other salad vegetables if desired.

This legendary dish is a speciality of the Issan region (north-east Thailand), and is often regarded rather nervously by *farangs* (Westerners). However, we once served it to a party of thirty Australians, many of whom were very conservative in their tastes, and it was greatly appreciated by all.

MAKEUA YAO PAD PRIK

FRIED EGGPLANT WITH BEEF AND CHILLIES

2 small eggplants (aubergines)
1 tablespoon oil
200 g lean beef, cut into short thin strips
2 cloves garlic, coarsely chopped
30 (approx.) fresh basil leaves
4 large mild chillies, cut into strips
1–2 tablespoons nam pla (fish sauce)
1 tablespoon brown sugar (optional)

This dish depends so much on the flavour of the fresh basil that it is not worth attempting unless you have some available.

Cut the eggplants into bite-size wedges, sprinkle with salt on both sides, and leave for 15 minutes. Wash and blot dry. Heat the oil in a wok or frypan and fry the beef and garlic over a high heat until the meat is browned. Add the eggplant and continue stirring for 5 minutes, adding a little water if it seems too dry. Add the basil leaves (whole) and the chillies, with *nam pla* and sugar to taste. Continue stirring, still on a high heat, until the eggplant is soft.

Meat and Poultry Dishes

NEUEA KEM

DRIED SALTY BEEF

500 g lean beef (rump)
1 tablespoon coriander seeds
1 tablespoon cumin seeds
4 tablespoons nam pla (fish sauce)
Oil for deep-frying

Cut the beef into slices about 2 cm x 4 cm and around 5 mm thick. Crush the coriander and cumin seeds together into coarse fragments (not powder). Add the *nam pla* and marinate the beef strips in the mixture for 1 hour. Lay the strips out on a tray and dry in the sun for about an hour, turning once. (This step can be omitted if inconvenient.) Fry the beef in deep oil in a wok until "half-crisp" — that is, crisp around the edges but still soft in the centre. This dish is commonly eaten as an accompaniment to a *gaeng* (curry).

There are two versions of this dish in Thailand. Traditional *neuea kem* would consist of thicker slices of beef marinated in *nam pla* only, and dried in the sun over several days until quite dry, like "jerky" or "biltong". It would be fried, then eaten cold with glutinous rice. The version given here would more strictly be called *neuea dad deeo* (one sun beef), and is the form that would be served with other dishes as part of a dinner menu.

NEUEA PAD TUA FAK YAO

BEEF WITH SNAKE BEANS

200 g snake beans OR green or French beans
1 tablespoon oil (for frying)
1 clove garlic, finely chopped
200 g rump steak, thinly sliced
$\frac{1}{2}$ teaspoon coriander seeds, crushed or ground
2 tablespoons nam pla (fish sauce)

Snake beans are a variety of green beans which grow to a length of 60 cm or more. They are fairly widely available but green beans or French beans could be substituted.

Top and tail the beans and cut them into pieces 7–8 cm long. Heat the oil in a wok or frypan and fry the garlic until brown. Throw in the steak, stirring, and when it has browned add the beans and ground coriander (we keep an additional peppermill with coriander seeds in it). Continue stirring and tossing over a high heat for 1 minute, then add the *nam pla*. Reduce the heat and stir for another 1–2 minutes until the beans are cooked but still crisp.

Meat and Poultry Dishes

PANANG NEUEA

MEATBALLS WITH PEANUT SAUCE

Meatballs:
500 g beef mince
Flour for dusting
2 tablespoons oil

Sauce:
1 tablespoon Kreung Gaeng Ped (red curry paste, see p. 42)
2 tablespoons raw peanuts, crushed OR crunchy peanut butter
1 cup thick coconut milk (see p. 7)
1 tablespoon nam pla (fish sauce)
2 teaspoons sugar, preferably palm or raw sugar

Garnish:
Basil leaves
Red chillies, cut into slivers

Roll the mince into 25 mm (1 inch) balls, and drop each into a bowl of flour to coat it lightly. Heat the oil in a wok or frypan and fry the meatballs, tossing and turning regularly, for about 10 minutes. They should be cooked through and crispy brown on the outside. Remove them from the oil and put them aside to drain.

Fry the curry paste in the remaining oil for 1–2 minutes, until it smells cooked. Add the peanuts and coconut milk and stir well. Bring to the boil and add the *nam pla* and sugar; adjust if necessary. Return the meatballs to the pan and simmer in the sauce for 5 minutes. The sauce should be quite thick; increase the heat for a minute or two if it is too thin. Serve garnished with basil leaves and, optionally, slivers of red chilli.

As well as a dish at a main meal, the meatballs could also be served (using cocktail sticks) as an appetiser before the meal.

MOO WAN

SWEET PORK

1 tablespoon oil
300 g pork fillet, sliced into small thin slices, about 1 cm x 2 cm and 2 mm thick
½ small onion, finely sliced lengthways
1 tablespoon dark soy sauce
4 tablespoons palm or brown sugar

Garnish:
Coriander leaves
Mild chillies, thinly sliced

Heat the oil in a wok or frypan, throw in the pork and the onion and stir continuously for 2 minutes or so, until the pork is browned on the surface. Add the soy sauce and the sugar, one spoonful at a time, stirring continually. Turn the heat down, and simmer for 10 minutes. Moisture will come out of the pork, so it is unnecessary to add any water. Garnish with coriander leaves and possibly also chillies.

In Thailand this dish (and most others requiring sugar) would use palm sugar, which has much more flavour than cane sugar.

Meat and Poultry Dishes

MOO KEM

SALT PORK

250 g pork, diced
100 mL water
2 teaspoons salt
1 tablespoon oil

Put the pork, water and salt in a frypan or wok. Bring to the boil and continue boiling until dry (taking care that it does not burn). Add the oil and stir-fry until browned.

This dish goes very well with *Nam Prik Gapi* (vegetables with hot sauce, see p. 81), but can also be served as a side-dish with almost any meal.

PAD DOK KANAH

PORK WITH BROCCOLI

1 tablespoon oil
1 clove garlic, finely chopped
100 g pork fillet, cut into thin strips
250 g broccoli, divided into small pieces
1 tablespoon nam pla (fish sauce)
4 tablespoons water

Fry the garlic in the oil in a wok or frypan until brown, then add the pork and stir-fry for 5 minutes. Add the broccoli, stir-fry for a further 3 minutes until it softens, then add the *nam pla* and water. Stir quickly while it sizzles then remove from the heat and serve.

Egg Dishes

Egg Dishes

KAI LOOK KOEI

SON-IN-LAW EGGS

6 eggs
Oil for frying
2 tablespoons dried onion flakes
3 tablespoons brown sugar
2 tablespoons nam pla (fish sauce)
2 tablespoons vinegar
Garnish:
Coriander leaves
Red chilli, cut into fine slivers

Boil the eggs "half-hard" for 8 minutes and cool immediately with cold water. Shell them and cut each in half lengthways. Cover the bottom of a big pan with 1 cm of oil and fry the halved eggs, yolk side down, over medium heat. Spoon the oil over the eggs as they fry. They must be removed as soon as they are browned and slightly blistered; frying them too long will make them rubbery. Arrange the eggs, yolk side up, on a serving dish.

Pour out the oil, leaving just enough to cover the bottom of the pan. Throw in the onion flakes, fry them for a second then remove them. With the heat low stir in the brown sugar, *nam pla* and vinegar. Adjust the sauce to taste — it should be a distinctive blend of sweet, salt and sour tastes. Let it come to the boil and pour it over the eggs immediately. Spread the onion flakes evenly over the top. Garnish with chilli and coriander.

KAI PALOH

EGGS WITH PORK

Roots of 4 coriander plants
Leaves of 1 coriander plant
2 cloves garlic
1 tablespoon oil
150 g pork, diced
3 tablespoons dark soy sauce
500 mL water
3 tablespoons brown sugar
4 hard-boiled eggs

Wash the coriander roots well and bruise them with the side of a cleaver or heavy knife, keeping them whole. Similarly, bruise the garlic. Fry the coriander roots and garlic in the oil, in a saucepan, for about 2 minutes, then add the meat and fry for a further 5 minutes. Add the soy sauce and stir-fry for 1 minute, then add the water and the sugar. Simmer until the meat is nearly cooked — 30 minutes for bite-size pieces, less if it is diced smaller — then add the peeled eggs and the coriander leaves and simmer a further 15 minutes.

This dish is a great favourite with children in Thailand — and in Australia too, at least in our family. The flavours are mild, but the combination is sufficiently "different" for adults to find it quite interesting too. In Western terms, *Kai Paloh* comes somewhere between a soup and a stew, but it is eaten with rice as one of the dishes at a main meal. It can be made with beef instead of pork. You do not eat the coriander roots — they are just there to flavour the sauce.

Egg Dishes

KAI GIO
THAI OMELETTE

2 eggs
1 teaspoon nam pla (fish sauce)
1 teaspoon water
Oil for frying

Beat the eggs with the *nam pla* and water. Heat enough oil to cover the bottom of a 20 cm frypan; when it is hot, tip in the eggs. As soon as the base of the omelette forms a skin, push it to one side of the pan with a spatula. Keeping that side away from the heat, let a new skin form, and repeat the process until all the mixture is cooked. Roll the omelette up and serve.

If the omelette is to be a dish in its own right it would often be eaten with *Nam Pla Prik* (spiced fish sauce, see p. 84) or *Nam Prik Siracha* (Siracha chilli sauce, see p. 84). An omelette is often served with *Gaeng Som* (sour soup, see p. 34). In Thailand one would often use duck eggs for *Kai Gio*.

KAI YAT SAI
STUFFED OMELETTE

Oil for frying
1 small onion, coarsely chopped
200 g minced pork or chicken
½ cup peas
1 tablespoon tomato paste
½ teaspoon salt
½ teaspoon sugar
3 eggs

Garnish:
Coriander leaves
Red chillies, finely sliced

Heat 1 tablespoon of oil in a frypan or wok and fry the onion until soft but not brown, then add the meat and fry until lightly browned. Add the peas, tomato paste, salt and sugar and continue frying gently until the peas and meat are cooked (5–10 minutes). Remove from the heat and set aside.

Beat the eggs. In a large frypan or wok, heat just enough oil to cover the bottom. (If you are using the same pan, make sure any residue of the filling is wiped out with kitchen tissue.) When the oil is really hot throw in the eggs and reduce the heat, tilting the pan so that the omelette spreads out into a thin layer and is as large as possible. When the base of the omelette is set, but the top is still softish, spoon the filling onto the centre. (If your omelette or your pan is too small, save some of the filling — you must leave sufficient omelette clear to fold right over the stuffing.) With a spatula, carefully fold four sides of the omelette over the filling, so that you end up with a square packet. If the top needs more heat to cook and seal it, brown it gently under the grill. Lift out carefully and serve garnished with coriander and red chilli.

Egg Dishes

KAI GIO MOO SUP
PORK OMELETTE

3 eggs
100 g minced pork
OR *chicken*
1 spring onion, chopped
1 tablespoon nam pla (fish sauce)
Oil for frying

Accompaniment:

Nam Pla Prik (spiced fish sauce, see p. 84)

Beat the eggs with the *nam pla*, then stir in the pork and the spring onion. Heat 1 tablespoon of oil in a medium frypan or wok, tip in the omelette mixture and tilt the pan so that the bottom is covered. When the base is set and the top is not too runny, flip the omelette over to cook the other side, adding a dribble more oil if necessary. (An easy way to turn it is to tip it onto a large plate then slide it back into the pan.) Serve with *Nam Pla Prik*.

This dish can be made with minced chicken, in which case it would be called *Kai Gio Gai Sup*.

KAI KEM
PICKLED EGGS

4 cups (1 L) water
150 g salt
12 eggs

Heat the water, stir in the salt and bring to the boil, then leave it to cool. Wash and dry the eggs. Arrange the eggs in a jar, cover them with the brine and cap tightly. Leave for at least 2 weeks — they will keep for up to a year.

Take out as many eggs as you want, and hard boil them before eating. They can be eaten as a savoury or snack, or as a light meal with plain *Kao Tom* (rice cooked until quite soft in excess water). Other accompaniments for such a light meal would be *Neuea Kem* (dried salty beef, p. 60) or *Moo Wan* (sweet pork, p. 61) and a bowl of dried shrimps with chopped chillies and onions, soused in *nam pla* (fish sauce) and a generous squeeze of lemon juice.

Egg Dishes

KAI CHOM CHAN
MOONGAZING EGGS

6 eggs
6 peppercorns
6 coriander roots
2 cloves garlic
100 g minced pork
100 g white fish fillet, finely chopped
*1 tablespoon nam pla (*fish sauce*)*
*Oil for frying (*about 4 tablespoons*)*

Garnish:

Coriander leaves
Red chillies

Boil the eggs half-hard (7–8 minutes), peel them and halve them lengthways. Pound the peppercorns, coriander roots and garlic together in a mortar and pestle, then mix in the pork and fish and pound again lightly. Remove the yolks from the eggs and mash the yolks into the mixture. Add the *nam pla* and mix well; if the mixture is too dry to handle add a few drops of water.

Stuff the mixture into the cavities left by the egg yolks, and form any surplus into a gentle mound over the cut side. Heat the oil in a frying pan or wok and fry the eggs cut side down over a medium heat until the filling is cooked (about 4 minutes) then turn them to brown the other side for a minute or two. Unless you have a very large pan we suggest frying 6 halves at a time. Garnish with coriander leaves and thinly sliced chillies.

Vegetable Dishes

Vegetable Dishes

PAD FUK TONG

FRIED PUMPKIN

Oil for frying
½ medium-sized butternut pumpkin, cut into thin slices (2 cm x 2 cm, 5 mm thick)
2 cloves garlic, coarsely chopped
1 tablespoon nam pla (fish sauce)
2 eggs

Garnish:

Coriander leaves
Nam Prik Siracha (Siracha chilli sauce, see p. 84)

Just cover the bottom of a pan with oil. When it is very hot throw in the pumpkin and the garlic. Add the *nam pla*. Stir and toss it continuously, over a high heat, until the pumpkin is soft. Make a well in the centre and break the eggs into it. Stir it around vigorously; the eggs will set virtually immediately. Turn off the heat.

Garnish with coriander leaves and serve with a separate dish of *Nam Prik Siracha*.

PAD GALUMBLEE

FRIED CABBAGE

1 tablespoon oil
1–2 tablespoons nam pla (fish sauce)
2 cloves garlic, coarsely chopped
½ small cabbage, sliced

Heat the oil in a wok; when it is hot add the *nam pla* (careful — it will spit) and the garlic. Keeping the heat high, fry the garlic for 1 minute then add the cabbage. Stir and turn continually over a high heat until the cabbage is soft (about 5 minutes).

PAD PAK BOONG

FRIED SWAMP CABBAGE

500 g (1 bunch) pak boong (swamp cabbage) OR spinach or silverbeet
1 tablespoon oil
3 cloves garlic, chopped
2 teaspoons black beans (tinned) (see p. 10)
3 tablespoon water

Pak boong is often available in Chinese supermarkets. Spinach or silverbeet (perpetual spinach) could be cooked in the same way.

Cut up the *pak boong* so that each leaf is separate with its own section of stalk. (The stalk is cooked, not discarded.) Heat the oil in a wok and throw in the *pak boong* and the garlic. Stirring, add the black beans then the water. Continue stirring until the *pak boong* is cooked — this will take 2 or 3 minutes.

PAD PAK GAD DONG

FRIED PICKLED CABBAGE

½ teaspoon oil
3 cloves garlic, coarsely chopped
200 g pickled cabbage (tinned or fresh) (see p. 36), thinly sliced
1 teaspoon sugar (see below)
1 egg

If you are using the sweet kind of pickled cabbage (which is correct for this dish), omit the sugar.

Heat the oil in a pan, add the garlic and stir-fry for 1 minute. Throw in the cabbage and the sugar; stir in well and cook for 3 minutes. Make a well in the centre and break the egg into it. Stir vigorously until the egg is cooked.

Vegetable Dishes

PAD MAKEUA YAO

FRIED EGGPLANT

250 g eggplant (aubergine) (1 large or 2 small)
1 clove garlic, finely chopped
1 tablespoon oil
1 chilli, cut into slivers
10 basil leaves
1 tablespoon black bean sauce
4 tablespoons water

Cut the eggplant into slices, sprinkle with salt and leave for 30 minutes. Rinse, dry and dice. Fry the garlic in the oil for 2–3 minutes, until brown, then throw in the eggplant and fry for 3 minutes, keeping the heat high. Add the chilli and the basil and fry a further 2 minutes. Stir in the black bean sauce and water, then remove from the heat.

PAD PAK KWANG TOONG

FRIED CHARD

½ tablespoon oil
3 cloves garlic, chopped
1 tablespoon oyster sauce
½ bunch (2 big plants) Swiss chard (buck choy), cut into pieces about 4 cm long

Chard or Swiss chard (kwangtoong) is commonly used in continental European cooking but is often found in shops under its Chinese name, buck choy, since Chinese food uses it a lot.

Heat the oil in a pan or wok and fry the garlic for 1 minute. Stir in the oyster sauce then add the chard and continue stirring until cooked.

PAD TUA SONG YANG

FRIED GREEN BEANS AND SPROUTS

½ tablespoon oil
1 large clove garlic, chopped
100 g green beans, cut into 3 cm pieces
1 tablespoon nam pla (fish sauce)
1 tablespoon oyster sauce
50 g bean sprouts

Heat the oil in a wok or frypan, throw in the garlic and green beans and stir-fry for about 2 minutes. Add the nam pla, oyster sauce and bean sprouts and continue stirring until cooked but still crisp (1 or 2 minutes).

KANAH PAD NAM MUN HOY

BROCCOLI WITH OYSTER SAUCE

1 tablespoon oil
200 g broccoli, cut into sprigs
2 tablespoons oyster sauce
2 tablespoons water

Heat the oil in a wok or frypan and add the broccoli. Toss over a high heat for 2 minutes, then add the oyster sauce and water. Reduce the heat a little and continue stirring for 2 or 3 minutes until the broccoli is becoming soft but not mushy.

Thai Salads
Yam

SOM TAM
(Green papaya salad), recipe page 78

YAM TALAE
(Seafood salad), recipe page 75

Thai Salads – Yam

YAM TALAE
SEAFOOD SALAD

4 dried chillies
$\frac{1}{2}$ teaspoon coriander seeds
5 peppercorns
7 tablespoons lemon juice
4 tablespoons nam pla (fish sauce)
1 tablespoon brown sugar
3 stalks lemon grass, chopped finely
300 mL water
500 g mixed raw seafood (marinara mix or mixed chopped squid, peeled small prawns and shelled shellfish)

Garnish:

Lettuce leaves, chopped
Coriander leaves

In a mortar, pound the chillies, coriander seeds and peppercorns to a coarse powder. Add the lemon juice, *nam pla*, sugar and lemon grass and mix well. Taste, and adjust if necessary with more sugar, lemon juice or *nam pla*.

Bring the water to the boil and throw in the seafood; remove from the heat and drain as soon as the water has come back to the boil.

Mix the seafood with the dressing and serve on a bed of chopped lettuce leaves, garnished with coriander leaves.

YAM GOONG HAENG
DRIED SHRIMP SALAD

3 tablespoons lemon juice
$1\frac{1}{2}$ tablespoons nam pla (fish sauce)
1 tablespoon brown sugar
1 or 2 hot chillies, chopped finely
1 teaspoon coriander seeds, crushed
$\frac{1}{2}$ teaspoon freshly ground pepper
$\frac{1}{2}$ cup dried shrimps

Suggested vegetables:

$\frac{1}{2}$ small lettuce, tomato, capsicum (bell pepper), carrot, coriander leaves, green apple, spring onions, radishes

These are only suggestions: lettuce or at least one leaf vegetable is essential, but virtually any vegetable and crisp-textured fruit can be included.

Mix the lemon juice, *nam pla*, sugar, chillies (including seeds), coriander and pepper. Taste and adjust as necessary — it should be sharp and hot. Add the dried shrimps, and leave to soak while you cut up the vegetables.

Cut, wash and arrange the vegetables, then tip the shrimps and dressing over them. Decorate, if you wish, with chillies and radishes cut into flowers.

Thai Salads – Yam

GOONG SANG WAH

PRAWNS FEIGNING DEAD

2–3 stalks lemon grass
$\frac{1}{2}$ small onion
2 spring onions
2 coriander plants
1 teaspoon fresh makrut (Kaffir lime) peel
1 chilli
5 sprigs mint
5 fresh makrut (Kaffir lime) leaves
2–3 cm piece fresh ginger, peeled
150 g green (raw) prawn meat (300 g whole prawns, peeled and de-veined, see p. 36)

Dressing:

1 tablespoon nam pla (fish sauce)
2 tablespoons lime juice
1 teaspoon palm sugar

Garnish:

Lettuce leaves

The *makrut* leaves and peel must be fresh, not dried — if you cannot obtain fresh makrut substitute lime or lemon peel and leaves. Similarly, pick the tenderest ginger roots and lemon grass you can, using the bottom 10–15 cm of the lemon grass shoots.

Chop the lemon grass, onion, spring onions, coriander (including the thinner stems) and *makrut* peel very finely. Remove the seeds from the chilli and cut into thin slices. Slice the mint, *makrut* leaves and ginger into slivers.

Cook the prawns lightly by placing them in a sieve and pouring boiling water over them — they will turn pink and lose their transparency almost immediately. Cut them into pieces and mix with all the chopped and sliced ingredients.

Mix the *nam pla*, lime juice and sugar; adjust to taste — it should be sharp and salty. Pour it over the prawn and herb mixture and stir well.

Serve on a bed of lettuce leaves.

YAM MAKEUA YAO PAO

EGGPLANT AND PORK SALAD

4 eggplants (aubergines)
100 g pork fillet, very thinly sliced
100 mL thick coconut milk (see p. 7)
$\frac{1}{4}$ cup dried shrimps
1 tablespoon raw peanuts
2 dried chillies
1 tablespoon nam pla (fish sauce)
2 tablespoons lemon juice
1 tablespoon sugar
$\frac{1}{2}$ small onion, finely sliced

Garnish:

Coriander leaves

The best eggplants for this are the long, thin, green ones, about the size and shape of cucumbers, but the purple kind can be used provided that they are not too large.

Grill the eggplants, whole, for about 10 minutes, turning from time to time. The skin should just be a little burnt and the flesh quite soft. With a sharp knife slit the skin of each eggplant and peel it while still hot. Cut the flesh into chunks and arrange on a plate.

Simmer the pork in the coconut milk until cooked (around 10 minutes). While it is cooking, pound the dried shrimps in a mortar and pestle until shredded and, separately, pound the peanuts and then the chillies (coarsely). Mix the *nam pla* with the lemon juice and sugar, and add the pounded chillies.

Spoon the pork and coconut milk over the arranged eggplants. Sprinkle the onion, the ground peanuts and then the shrimps in layers on top, then pour the dressing over. Garnish with coriander leaves.

Thai Salads – Yam

YAM NANG MOO

PORK SKIN SALAD

125 g piece pork skin
1 clove garlic, chopped
1 teaspoon oil
125 g minced pork
50 mL (2½ tablespoons) lime juice (juice of one lime) or lemon juice
2 teaspoons palm (or brown) sugar
1 tablespoon nam pla (fish sauce)
1 small hot (birdseye) chilli, finely chopped
½ small onion, finely sliced
2 tablespoons raw peanuts, chopped or coarsely crushed
2 coriander plants

Garnish:

Lettuce leaves
Coriander leaves

You can buy pork skin from Chinese butchers, but we prefer to use the skin from pork used for other dishes — it will keep in the freezer until required. The recipe can easily be adjusted to suit the amount of skin you have available.

Put the pork skin into a saucepan of cold water and bring to the boil, then simmer until soft (about 1 hour). Leave to cool in the water. When cool, remove any fat and slice the skin into thin strips, about 3 mm wide and 3–5 cm long.

Fry the garlic in the oil, in a wok, until golden. Remove the garlic and put aside, then tip out the oil. Fry the minced pork in the wok, without adding any extra oil or water, until cooked (5 minutes or so).

In a bowl, prepare the dressing. Mix the lime (or lemon) juice, sugar and *nam pla*. Taste and adjust as necessary — it should be a little sharp, but with a balance of all three flavours. (Limes and lemons vary in sourness, and fish sauces also differ, so the proportions given can only be a guide.) Add the chilli (without the seeds if you do not want the *yam* to be too hot) to the sauce, then the pork skin, minced pork, onion, peanuts and the leaves of a good-sized coriander plant. Mix well, cover, and leave to marinate in the refrigerator for at least 1 hour.

Serve on a bed of lettuce leaves with the reserved fried garlic sprinkled over the top, and garnished with more coriander leaves.

YAM KAI TOM

THAI EGG SALAD

3 eggs
1 capsicum (bell pepper) OR *2 banana chillies*
3 spinach leaves OR *100 g pak boong (swamp cabbage)*
1 tablespoon dried shrimps, pounded (optional)
Juice of 1 lime (approx. 50 mL)
2 teaspoons sugar
1½ tablespoons nam pla (fish sauce)

Boil the eggs for 10 minutes, peel them and cut them into quarters. Grill the capsicum until soft then cut it into thin strips. Line a dish with washed spinach leaves. (If using *pak boong*, blanch the leaves with boiling water first.) Arrange the capsicum strips and quartered eggs attractively and sprinkle the dried shrimps on top. Mix the lime juice, sugar and *nam pla*, adjust to taste and pour it over the salad.

Thai Salads – Yam

SOM TAM

GREEN PAPAYA SALAD

1 unripe papaya OR *500 g carrot, grated (see below)*
3 cloves garlic
5 peppercorns
2 small hot (birdseye) chillies
10 cherry tomatoes
1 tablespoon sugar
Juice of 2 limes or 1 lemon
2 tablespoons nam pla (fish sauce)
2 tablespoons roasted peanuts, crushed
2 tablespoons dried shrimps, coarsely pounded

Suggested raw vegetables:

lettuce leaves, snake beans, pak boong (swamp cabbage) tips, Chinese cabbage leaves.

Peel and seed the papaya and grate the flesh into long, thin shreds. (As a poor substitute, you could use 500 grams of carrots, peeled and grated.)

In a mortar, pound the garlic and peppercorns together to a coarse paste. Add the chillies, whole, and pound them into the paste. Add the tomatoes, and pound gently to break the fruits and release their pulp while keeping each one more or less in one piece. (To make the *yam* less hot add the chillies after the tomatoes, and only crush them lightly.) Add the *nam pla* and lime juice, then stir in the sugar until it is dissolved. Adjust to taste — it should be sharp and hot, and subtly sweet and salty. Next, add the peanuts, then the papaya and half the shrimps, and mix thoroughly.

Serve on a shallow dish which has been lined with lettuce leaves. Sprinkle the remaining dried shrimps on top. Eat it with a selection of raw vegetables.

This *yam* is often served as part of a lunch menu, with *Kao Mun* (rice cooked in coconut milk, see p. 25), *Gaeng Ped Gai* (red curry of chicken, see p. 44) and *Neuea Kem* (dried salty beef, see p. 60).

Hot Sauce Dishes
Nam prik

Hot Sauce Dishes – *Nam prik*

NAM PRIK GAPI
VEGETABLES WITH HOT SAUCE

Sauce:

1 teaspoon onion, coarsely chopped
2 cloves garlic
10 peppercorns
1 teaspoon dried shrimps, pounded
3 red birdseye chillies (to taste)
Juice of 2 limes (or 1 lemon)
1 tablespoon palm (or brown) sugar
2 teaspoons gapi (shrimp paste)

Some suggested vegetables:

Raw vegetables: lettuce leaves, sliced carrot, tomato segments, sliced apple, cucumber, radishes, cauliflower sprigs.

Cooked vegetables: snake beans (or green beans), okra, asparagus tips

Using a mortar and pestle, pound the onion, garlic and peppercorns to a coarse paste. Add the dried shrimps and chillies, continue pounding. Add the lime juice and the sugar, still pounding, and finally the *gapi*. Mix to an even consistency. Adjust the seasoning if necessary — it should be slightly sharp and very hot. Serve in a small bowl in the centre of a large plate, surrounded with a selection of raw and cooked vegetables.

Cook the vegetables in thin coconut milk until just tender (5 minutes).

A "basic" *nam prik* like this, with rice, would often be the evening meal for a not too well-off Thai family; it is regarded to some extent as "peasant food". Nevertheless the better-off would not be too proud to include it as one of the dishes in a more elaborate meal — though many Thais are nervous of serving this pungent sauce to *farangs* (Westerners).

NAM PRIK PLA THU
HOT SAUCE WITH MACKEREL

2–4 pla thu (mackerel, yellowtail)
Salt
Oil for deep-frying
Nam Prik Gapi (vegetables with hot sauce, see p. 81)

A more substantial *nam prik* would have fish as well as the hot sauce and vegetables. The typical fish for this purpose is *pla thu*, a small variety of mackerel (*Rastrelliger chrysozonus* and related species). In Thailand one would buy them from the market already steamed, and just fry them before serving. They are commonly only 15 to 20 cm long, and if you are using larger mackerel only one or two would be required.

Clean the mackerel, rub them generously with salt and cook in a steamer (or a sieve or colander in a saucepan of boiling water) for 5 minutes. This can be done in advance (and should be, if you intend keeping them more than a few hours). Deep-fry in a wok, in enough oil to cover, until the skin is crisp, turning once. Serve with the vegetables arranged around and the sauce in a separate dish.

Smoked mackerel, which is ready to eat as bought, makes a very acceptable (and effortless) substitute for *pla thu*, even if it is not totally authentic.

Hot Sauce Dishes – *Nam prik*

NAM PRIK MAMUANG

GREEN MANGO HOT SAUCE

1 teaspoon onion, coarsely chopped
2 cloves garlic
10 peppercorns
3 red birdseye chillies (to taste)
1 teaspoon dried shrimps, pounded
1 tablespoon palm (or brown) sugar
2 teaspoons gapi (shrimp paste)
$\frac{1}{2}$ green (unripe) mango, finely grated

Pound the onion, garlic and peppercorns to a paste; add the chillies and dried shrimps, still pounding, then the sugar. When all is well pounded stir in the *gapi* and the mango.

Serve with vegetables as for *Nam Prik Gapi* (vegetables with hot sauce, see p. 81), but including young mango leaves in the raw vegetables.

This variant on the basic *nam prik gapi* will be particularly interesting to those living in tropical regions who have mango trees in their gardens or nearby. Mango leaves have a peppery taste, and watercress or nasturtium leaves would make an adequate substitute for those in cooler climates.

NAM JIM

DIPPING CHILLI SAUCE

300 g mild red chillies
20 g garlic (4–6 cloves)
1 cup vinegar
3 tablespoons granulated (white) sugar
4 teaspoons salt

Make as *Nam Prik Siracha* (see p. 84), but leave the seeds in the chillies. Give the mixture only a short buzz in the blender and do not strain. "Dipping sauce" is quite thick and chunky, and considerably hotter than Siracha sauce.

NAM PRIK ONG

PORK HOT SAUCE

Sauce:
1 stalk lemon grass, finely chopped
2 dried chillies, soaked
1 teaspoon salt
1 small onion, chopped
5 cloves garlic
1 teaspoon gapi (shrimp paste)
12 cherry tomatoes
100 g minced pork
1 tablespoon oil
$\frac{1}{2}$ cup water
1 tablespoon tamarind water (see p. 11) OR $\frac{1}{2}$ teaspoon tamarind concentrate

Accompaniments:
Dipping vegetables
Pork crackling

In a mortar, pound the lemon grass, chillies and salt. Add the onion, with 3 peeled cloves of garlic, and continue pounding to a fine paste. Add the *gapi* and pound in with the pestle. Add the tomatoes and pound in, then mix in the minced pork. Chop the 2 remaining cloves of garlic, heat the oil in a saucepan and fry the garlic until brown. Add the contents of the mortar and continue frying for about 3 minutes. Add the water and tamarind and simmer until thick — it should be the consistency of a dip rather than a soup.

Serve *Nam Prik Ong* with fresh, raw vegetables, such as those suggested for *Nam Prik Gapi* (see p. 81). The other essential accompaniment is crispy pork crackling — a packet from the supermarket would do, but if you have some pork skin, cut it into strips and deep-fry until puffy. (Next time you cook pork chops, do not throw the skin away — save it in the freezer for *Nam Prik Ong* or *Yam Nang Moo* (pork skin salad, see p. 77).)

Hot Sauce Dishes – *Nam prik*

NAM PRIK PAO
ROAST HOT SAUCE

10 cloves garlic
1 medium onion
10 dried small chillies
150 mL oil
2½ tablespoons dried shrimps
2 teaspoons nam pla (fish sauce)
2½ tablespoons palm (or brown) sugar
Pinch salt
1 tablespoon tamarind water (see p. 11)
3 teaspoons gapi (shrimp paste)

Finely slice the garlic and onion, and spread out on a plate to dry (in the sun, if possible) for 1–2 hours. It should not be totally desiccated. Chop the chillies, removing the seeds if you do not want the *Nam Prik Pao* to be too hot. Heat the oil in a wok or pan and fry the onion until golden. Remove it, then fry the garlic until brown. Remove this, and fry the shrimps and the chillies in turn. Let all the ingredients cool, and strain the oil to remove any bits and pieces. Mix the *nam pla*, sugar, salt and tamarind water, and stir until dissolved. In a mortar, pound the onion, garlic and chillies to a fine paste. Add the shrimps and continue pounding until they are reduced to the same consistency. Mix in the *gapi*.

Heat the oil again and fry the paste until aromatic (see p. 41), then tip in the *nam pla* mixture. Simmer for 2 or 3 minutes and adjust sugar, *nam pla* or tamarind to taste if necessary. Store in a jar with a tight-fitting lid, in the refrigerator.

Nam Prik Pao is more of a spread than a dip. It can be eaten with rice, or spread on bread or biscuits, or in a sandwich. It can be used in small quantities as a dip with prawn crackers, pork crackling or fried dried rice patties (*kao tang*). It is also used as an ingredient in cooked dishes (see *Tom Yam Goong*, p. 36). You can often buy it in jars in shops which sell Thai food, but homemade is always tastier!

TAO JIEW LON
YELLOW BEAN DIP

1 onion
2 tablespoons tinned yellow (soy) beans (see p. 10)
200 mL thick coconut milk (see p. 7)
100 g minced pork
100 g chopped raw prawn meat
1 teaspoon sugar
3 tablespoons tamarind water (see p. 11)
3 red chillies
Salt to taste

Accompaniments:

Fresh raw vegetables
Boiled rice (see p. 23)

Peel the onion. Slice half finely; cut the other half into small pieces and pound it in a mortar with the yellow beans. Heat the coconut milk in a saucepan until the oil begins to separate, add the minced pork and prawns and stir until cooked (around 10 minutes). Add the yellow bean mix and the sliced onion and stir. Add the sugar and tamarind water; taste and add salt if necessary (some brands of tinned yellow beans are more salty than others). Finally, add the chillies (whole) and simmer for 5–10 minutes.

Serve with a selection of fresh raw vegetables and, of course, plenty of boiled rice.

Hot Sauce Dishes – *Nam prik*

NAM PRIK SIRACHA

SIRACHA CHILLI SAUCE

300 g mild red chillies
30 g garlic (6–8 cloves)
1 cup vinegar
4 tablespoons granulated (white) sugar
4 teaspoons salt

Halve the chillies lengthways and remove the seeds. Peel the garlic and cut any particularly large cloves in half. Steam the chilli and garlic for 30 minutes in a steamer, or a sieve in a saucepan. Chop both very coarsely, cover with the vinegar and leave to soak overnight. Blend the chillies, garlic and vinegar in a liquidiser and strain into a saucepan, pressing as much as possible through the sieve. Add the sugar and salt, bring to the boil and simmer for 10–15 minutes until it begins to thicken.

Bottle in jars which have been sterilised in a saucepan of boiling water. The quantities given here make about 400 mL of sauce, which will just fill a 450 g jam jar; if you have plenty of chillies you can of course scale it up and make several jars to store.

This is not a dip but a sweet and not too hot chilli sauce. It can be eaten with almost anything — we recommend it specifically in some recipes, but a dish of it on the table will never be out of place. For a simple additional dish in a Thai menu, try a plate of plain cooked prawns, crab or crayfish with a dish of *Nam Prik Siracha*.

Siracha is a small but busy fishing and maritime town at the head of the Gulf of Siam, about 100 km from Bangkok. It is famous for its chilli sauce but we remember it more for a picturesque boat trip to the nearby island of Sichang. The boat was a barge with no seats, into which we (with our baby son) were crammed along with a motley variety of livestock, cargo and people, and which stopped at every little island in the bay before reaching our destination.

The evening boat back was more comfortable, being a passenger ferry only — an extraordinarily long, narrow boat with a canopy over it. A jar of Siracha sauce always brings back memories of that day!

NAM PLA PRIK

SPICED FISH SAUCE

5 small hot (birdseye) chillies
2 tablespoons nam pla (fish sauce)
Few drops lime or lemon juice

Cut the chillies crosswise into rings and add to the *nam pla* in a small dish. Add a few drops of lime or lemon juice — just enough to give a slight sharpness. Some people would add half a clove of garlic, chopped, especially with seafood dishes.

A Thai table always has a little bowl of *nam pla prik* on it, just as a Western one usually has a salt cellar, and for the same purpose — to add extra saltiness if required. It does not add much heat — unless you take one of the chilli pieces!

PRIK NAM SOM

CHILLIES IN VINEGAR

2 large mild chillies (1 red, 1 green if possible)
$\frac{1}{4}$ tablespoon salt
3 tablespoons vinegar

Cut the chillies crosswise into slices, without removing the seeds. Put them in a small bowl with the salt and vinegar.

Desserts and Sweets

Desserts and Sweets

KAO NEOW MAMUANG
GLUTINOUS RICE WITH MANGO

250 g glutinous rice
1 cup thick coconut milk (see below)
50 mL water
5 tablespoons sugar
½ teaspoon salt
6 fresh mangoes

Glutinous rice (*kao neow*) is a variety of rice which is sticky when cooked. It is normally used for desserts, though in the mountainous regions of North Thailand it is used instead of long grain rice with meals. Any Asian grocery will have it, and you might also find it in a health food store.

Soak the glutinous rice in cold water for at least 5 hours — preferably overnight. Rinse well, then cook in a steamer lined with muslin or a clean tea towel (so that the rice does not fall through the holes) for about 15 minutes or so, until cooked. Do not over-cook. (The time will depend very much on the shape and size of your steamer.) If you have no steamer you could improvise with a sieve or colander in a large saucepan (with a sieve, of course, the muslin is unnecessary).

Set aside 100 mL of the coconut milk. (If you are preparing coconut milk from fresh coconut or creamed coconut, make it rather thicker than normal thick milk by using less water.) Add the water, sugar and salt to the remainder of the coconut milk and warm in a saucepan until dissolved. Mix this with the rice and leave to cool. Add a pinch of salt to the reserved coconut milk and gently bring to the boil, stirring constantly. This will be the topping for the rice; keep it in a jug in the refrigerator until you serve it.

Peel and slice the mangoes, and serve a portion of rice on each plate surrounded by mango slices. Pour a little of the topping over each.

Kao Neow Mamuang is a classic Thai dessert, and during the mango season street stalls and itinerant vendors selling it are ubiquitous. *Kao neow* is also eaten with other desserts — topped with *Sankaya* (coconut custard, see p. 88), for example. If you cannot get fresh mangoes you could serve it with tinned mango slices, but of course this is not quite the same.

GLUAY BUAT CHEE
NUN BANANAS

2 cups thick coconut milk (see p. 7)
4 tablespoons white sugar
Pinch of salt
Few drops jasmine or vanilla essence
4 bananas, sliced

Warm the coconut milk with the sugar, a pinch of salt and a few drops of jasmine or vanilla essence. When the sugar has dissolved add the bananas and bring to the boil, stirring continuously. Simmer, still stirring, for just 30 seconds. Serve either hot or chilled.

The name means literally "bananas enter the convent as nuns" and refers to the white robes which a Thai Buddhist nun wears. "*Buat*" (to enter a convent) is used to describe any dish "robed in white" with sweetened coconut milk.

Desserts and Sweets

ICE-CREAM KATI SOD
COCONUT-MILK ICE-CREAM

200 g granulated (white) sugar
1 cup thick coconut milk (see below)
1½ cups thin coconut milk (see p. 7)
½ cup evaporated milk

Garnish:

Roasted (unsalted) peanuts, chopped
Sweet corn (cooked and scraped from the cob, or tinned corn kernels)

For the very best results you cannot beat fresh coconut for this recipe. Use 3 cups of freshly grated coconut, and two cups of boiling water. Soak all the coconut in half a cup of water at a time; squeeze out the milk then repeat with the next half cup, and so on. Alternatively, one 400 mL tin of coconut milk and 200 mL of water will provide an adequate substitute.

Mix the sugar and coconut milk and stir over a low heat until the sugar is all dissolved, then remove from the heat. Whip the evaporated milk until thick, and fold in the sweetened coconut milk. Tip into an ice-cream machine, if you have one, and churn until frozen (the quantity given will fit a 1 litre ice-cream maker); otherwise pour into a dish and put in the freezer (on a cold setting). Remove after 1 hour and stir well. After 2 hours, if it is still not fully frozen, stir again.

Serve sprinkled with chopped, roasted (unsalted) peanuts and/or sweet corn.

SANKAYA
COCONUT CUSTARD

6 eggs
200 g palm (or raw) sugar
400 mL thick coconut milk (see p. 7)

Beat the eggs and stir in the sugar until dissolved. Pour in the coconut milk and stir well. Pour into 6 individual custard dishes. Bring water to boil in a steamer; place the custard dishes in (3 at a time if your steamer is not large enough) and steam until set (about 20 minutes). Chill before serving.

If you do not have a suitable steamer, any large flat pan with a lid — even an electric skillet — would do, but take great care that the water neither boils over into the custard dishes nor boils dry.

The quantity given here makes 6 servings, but it can easily be scaled to suit your requirements. It can be eaten on its own, or served with *Kao Neow* (glutinous rice, see p. 87). In Thailand it might also be cooked in halved green coconuts (hard ripe coconuts are not suitable) or halved baby pumpkins. If you are trying this, increase the sugar to 250 g to compensate for the unsweetened pumpkin or coconut.

Desserts and Sweets

WOON GATI

TWO-TONE JELLY

Bottom layer:

3 tablespoons woon (agar-agar)
3 cups water
1 cup sugar
1 teaspoon pandanus essence

Top layer:

2 tablespoons woon (agar-agar)
2 cups thick coconut milk (see p. 7)
$\frac{1}{2}$ cup sugar
1 teaspoon salt

Agar-agar is made from seaweed, and can be bought from Asian shops and from most health food stores. It comes either in granulated form or as strips — if you have the strips chop them as finely as possible.

Make the clear, lower layer first. Mix the agar with the cold water in a saucepan, and let it soak for 2–3 minutes, then heat very slowly to boiling, stirring occasionally. Add the sugar and bring back to the boil, then stir in the pandanus essence. Pour into a flat tray or individual jelly moulds (even a cupcake tray), taking care not to fill more than half full. Leave it to cool and set. Allow at least 30 minutes and not more than 1 hour before pouring on the top layer; if it is too well set the two layers will not stick together.

To make the top layer, mix the agar and the coconut milk in a saucepan, and again allow to soak for 2–3 minutes. (If you are using tinned coconut milk, you could use one 400 mL tin and add 100 mL water to make up the 2 cups, rather than opening two tins — tinned coconut milk is always quite thick.) Add the sugar, then bring slowly to the boil, stirring frequently. Simmer gently, if necessary, until the sugar and agar are all dissolved, then add the salt. Stir well and pour on top of the clear layer. Leave until set. If made in a tray, cut into squares. Turn out

and serve (garnished with rose petals if you want the final authentic touch).

Other flavours can replace the pandanus — coffee, vanilla and caramel all make interesting alternatives. Whichever you use, they will disappear very fast if there are children about.

WOON SANKAYA

CUSTARD JELLY

$1\frac{1}{2}$ cups sheet agar-agar soaked in water for about 5 minutes then drained (about 2 tablespoons powdered agar)
3 cups water
$\frac{1}{2}$ cup granulated (white) sugar
$\frac{1}{2}$ cup palm sugar
1 cup thick coconut milk
3 eggs
1 teaspoon vanilla essence

Bring the water and agar to the boil, stirring often, then add the sugar. When it is all dissolved remove from the heat. Dissolve the palm sugar in the coconut milk and strain through a fine sieve. Lightly beat the eggs then add the sweetened coconut milk and mix thoroughly.

Put the agar mixture back on the heat and pour in the egg and coconut milk mixture. Stir *constantly* and turn off the heat just before it comes to the boil. Stir in the vanilla essence, pour into moulds and leave to cool and set.

Different forms of agar are rather variable, so the safest way to measure it is to soak it first. If the final mixture is heated too much it will curdle; this will spoil the appearance but will not harm the taste too much.

Desserts and Sweets

MAPROW GAEO

GLASS COCONUT

1 large coconut
2 cups granulated (white) sugar
1 cup water
Pandanus or other flavour essence (see below)
Red and green food colouring

Pandanus essence is a natural extract from the pandanus palm, and is available from many Asian supermarkets. You could use peppermint, vanilla or any other flavour essence — matching, naturally, the colour to the flavour.

Extract the coconut meat and grate it with a medium-sized grater, making the strands as long and thin as you can. Measure the grated coconut — you should have about 4 cups — adjust the other ingredients to suit if you have much more or less.

Divide the grated coconut into two halves. Mix 1 cup sugar and $\frac{1}{2}$ cup water in a saucepan, and gently bring to the boil, stirring continuously. Boil until a drop dripped into a saucer of iced water sets and becomes toffee-like. Immediately tip in one half of the coconut, with a few drops of pandanus (or other) flavouring and a few drops of green colouring, and stir in well. Some liquid will come out of the coconut — continue simmering until the syrup is back to its former syrupy consistency and is virtually all absorbed into or onto the coconut.

Spoon out individual heaped tablespoonfuls onto a greased baking tray and leave to cool. Repeat the process with the remaining half of the coconut, sugar and water, using red food colouring (and, if you like, a different flavour essence). When cool, serve in a dish as sweets.

If you boil the syrup for too long the sugar will crystallise on cooling and not look glassy, but it will still taste good. If you do not boil enough it will not set — but all is not lost. Put the baking tray into a cool oven (100°C) and leave for 30–40 minutes, and it will set on cooling.

MUN TOM NAM TAN

SWEET POTATOES IN GINGER SYRUP

2 cups water
1½ cups sugar
5 cm piece green ginger, peeled and finely sliced
600 g sweet potatoes, peeled and diced (3 cm cubes)

Mix the sugar with the water and slowly bring to the boil. Add the ginger and sweet potatoes, bring back to the boil and simmer for 15 minutes, or until the sweet potatoes are cooked.

Serve chilled or at room temperature.

NAM PRIK PLA THU
(Hot sauce with mackerel), recipe page 81

ICE-CREAM KATI SOD
(Coconut-milk ice-cream), recipe page 88

and **MAPROW GAEO**
(Glass coconut), recipe page 90

Desserts and Sweets

TA GOA HAEW

WATER-CHESTNUT CUPS

Base:
$\frac{1}{2}$ cup rice flour $\frac{1}{4}$ cup tapioca flour   } (see p. 8) 2 tablespoons bean (soya) flour
$2\frac{1}{2}$ cups water
1 teaspoon pandanus essence
$1\frac{1}{2}$ cups granulated (white) sugar
1 cup diced tinned water chestnuts
30 greaseproof paper cake cups

Topping:
400 mL thick coconut milk
100 mL water
$\frac{1}{4}$ cup rice flour
1 teaspoon salt

Mix the three flours together then stir in $1\frac{1}{2}$ cups of the water, a little at a time, and the pandanus essence. Ensure that all is well mixed. In a saucepan, bring the sugar and the remaining 1 cup of water to the boil and pour in the flour mixture. Bring back to the boil, over a medium to high heat, stirring often. As soon as it boils reduce the heat and continue stirring until the mixture is quite thick and stiff (about 15–20 minutes). Add the water chestnuts and mix in well, then quickly spoon into the cake cups, three-quarter filling each one.

Mix all the ingredients for the topping. Bring to the boil on a medium heat and continue cooking until the flour is cooked and the mixture thickens. Do not overcook or the coconut milk will separate. Very quickly fill up the cups with the topping, and cool until set.

The task of filling the cups is made easier if they are stood in cake tins which fit them neatly. In Thailand cups made of pandanus leaves would be used. *Ta goa* sets semi-solid, like blancmange, and is perhaps easiest to eat with a spoon.

Glossary

Various cooking and other terms crop up frequently in these pages, so here is a short list of what they mean. (This list does not include ingredients given on pp. 6–11.)

bai	leaf	*kai*	egg	*pad*	stir-fried	*som*	orange, or sharp-tasting
chee	nun	*kao* (rising tone)	white	*pak*	vegetable		
chud	bland	*kao* (falling tone)	rice	*pao*	roast	*tam*	pounded
daeng	red	*keo*	green	*ped*	hot (spicy)	*tom*	boiled
farang Westerner (also a guava, presumably because of its pale colour)		*krok*	mortar	*pla*	fish	*tord*	deep-fried
		look	child or seed	*prik*	chilli or pepper	*wan*	sweet
		moo	pork	*prio*	sour	*woon*	jelly
gai	chicken	*nam*	water, juice or sauce	*ron*	hot (temperature)		
goong	prawn	*neuea*	beef	*sark*	pestle		

Weights and Measures

Metric quantities are used exclusively in this book. For those used to Imperial or American measurements, the following tables give some useful equivalents. **All values are approximate**, but accurate enough for our recipes.

Some cooks like to measure dry ingredients by cups, while others prefer to use weight, so the following conversions may be useful:

1 cup flour = 150 g
1 cup sugar = 200 g
1 cup rice = 225 g

WEIGHT
(converted to the nearest 5 g)

metric	Imperial
30 g	1 oz
100 g	$3\frac{1}{2}$ oz
115 g	4 oz
225 g	8 oz ($\frac{1}{2}$ lb)
250 g	9 oz
455 g	1 lb
500 g	1 lb $1\frac{1}{2}$ oz
1 kg	2 lb 3 oz

LENGTH

metric	Imperial
3 mm	$\frac{1}{8}$ inch
6 mm	$\frac{1}{4}$ inch
1 cm	$\frac{3}{8}$ inch
2 cm	$\frac{3}{4}$ inch
2.5 cm	1 inch
5 cm	2 inches

VOLUME

(all cup and spoon measures are level)

volume	metric cup/spoon	Imperial cup/spoon	US cup/spoon	Imperial pints	US quarts	fluid oz.
5 mL	1 teaspoon	1 teaspoon	1 teaspoon			
15 mL			1 tablespoon			$\frac{1}{2}$
20 mL	1 tablespoon	1 tablespoon				
100 mL						1
125 mL	$\frac{1}{2}$ cup		$\frac{1}{2}$ cup			4
150 mL		$\frac{1}{2}$ cup				5
250 mL	1 cup	$\frac{3}{4}$ cup	1 cup		$\frac{1}{4}$	8
300 mL		1 cup		$\frac{1}{2}$		10
500 mL	2 cups	$1\frac{2}{3}$ cups	2 cups		$\frac{1}{2}$	16
600 mL		2 cups		1		20
1 L	4 cups	$3\frac{1}{3}$ cups	4 cups		1	32

Index